But He Looks So *Normal*!
A Bad-Tempered Parenting Guide for Foster Parents & Adopters

By Sarah Naish

First published 2016 by Amazon

Copyright © Sarah Naish 2016

ISBN: 13:978-1533671523

Dedicated to my exceptionally patient husband, Ray, and my formidable, brave, hardly ever bad-tempered children

ALSO BY THE AUTHOR

'Therapeutic Parenting in a Nutshell- Positives and Pitfalls' Amazon 2016: *A guide for adopters, foster carers and supporting professionals caring for traumatised children.*

Children's Books – Therapeutic Parenting Series
'William Wobbly and the Very Bad Day'
'Sophie Spikey has a Very Big Problem'
'Rosie Rudey and the Very Annoying Parent'
'Charley Chatty and the Wiggly Worry Worm'
(Co-authored with Rosie Jefferies. Published by Jessica Kingsley Publishers October 2016).

Introduction

I think I have *nearly* made the transition from a Bad-Tempered Mother to a Therapeutic Parent. *My children* think I am a Very Annoying Parent because I meet mad lying with incontrovertible truth, high drama with pointy-eyebrow-raising and bossy rudeness with steadfast refusals to be insulted.

When I go around the country training foster carers, adopters, other therapeutic parents and social workers, they are always THRILLED to hear about how I messed up (in my own parenting), often.

Yes, ok, my 5 adopted children turned out all right in the end, and on the way we learnt A LOT about therapeutic parenting. At the start, however, there was mostly bad-tempered, rude shoutyness laced with a heavy dose of sarcasm.

Not from the children you understand.

Gradually, over the years, the therapeutic parenting days became more frequent and the bad-tempered, shouty (screamy) ones less prevalent.

Sometimes therapeutic parents worry about the bad days, about 'losing it'....they might even fret about driving away and leaving their Arguing Children standing on the side of the motorway.

Maybe that last one was just me?

My five children contributed superbly to my swift descent into bad-tempered motherhood. I have decided to honestly share all the blunders made by Patronising Professionals, the propensity of others to make a difficult situation worse, and the challenges I have encountered during my parenting of my often tricky, children. To all the people who actually said to me over the years: **"But he looks so normal!"** - You know who you are.

I am not a bad-tempered *person*, only a Bad-Tempered *Mother*. I do not have enough time to ask people nicely to do things.

Maybe, a long time ago, I did ask my children nicely to do things. I don't remember that day. Maybe, one day I got bored of asking nicely 42,000 times and decided to just shout a shrill order instead. That seemed to work better, so now I cut out the 42,000 polite requests and move straight to the shrill bad-tempered screech.

People say I am a 'Bad-Tempered Mother.' Well if I am, at least I am a Bad-Tempered Mother (BTM) who has a bit of free time now.

This book is not *just* about parenting children who are adopted, fostered or have additional needs, such as ADHD, Autism etc. For all the differences in the ways we need to parent, there are many similarities when it comes to dealing with the day-to-day annoyances. Some stories in particular though, may resonate with adopters and foster parents. I might mention here for example, 'nonsense chatter' and 'duct tape' in the same sentence.

Happily, my children have all now (hurriedly) left home, providing me with the physical and emotional time to finally write up my diary entries and reflections from the last 18 years. Along the way I learnt about becoming a Therapeutic Parent, but in order to get there I had to make a lot of mistakes and live through Bad - Tempered Motherhood first!

So here it is - a catalogue of disasters with multiple examples of bad parenting; including all the other annoying things which have contributed to my bad-temperedness and exasperation over the years. If you want to know how to repel the 'But he looks so normal' Patronising Professional, the 'Baking -Mother-with-Clipboard, and nosy parents asking inappropriate questions, then this has been written for you.

Enjoy some quick fixes to make your lives easier and to dismiss the annoying people and tasks, as well as swiftly deal with the behavioural challenges so thoughtfully provided by your children (in a therapeutic- parenting-fail way).

At the very least, you will enjoy a good laugh and lose the gnawing doubt that no one else is quite as bad-tempered as you are.

Sarah Naish *(self-confessed Bad-Tempered Mother)*
July 2016

Quiz: Which Parent Are You?

I've notice that most parents <u>are</u> actually quite bad-tempered. They say things like, 'I never lost my temper before I had children,' or, 'I never even raised my voice before I had kids.'

Most mothers *appear* to be 'Perfect Mothers' or at least 'Good Mothers', but they are just working harder at hiding their bad temper, weariness and sense of having been deceived or cheated somehow. This is clearly illustrated in the table below:

Family types per 100 population UK

	Description	Percentage
BTM	Bad-Tempered Mother	69%
GM	Good Mothers	12%
PM	Perfect Mothers	1% (but media represents as 95%)
BMWC	Baking-Mother-With-Clipboard	8%
CM	Competitive Mothers	10%
PH	Patient Husband	n/a
INP	Ignorant Non Parent	100% of non-parents
IRT	Incredibly Rude Teenager	99% of all teenagers

Source: Sarah Naish's own personal experience and view

Try this quick quiz to see where you fall between perfection and bad-temperedness. (NB- Therapeutic Parents, make tea first).

1) Your child is off to school. Are they wearing:
   a) Perfectly matched, shiny white socks?
   b) Socks that appear to match?
   c) Not sure, have they gone to school?

2) Your child is in the school play. Do you:
   a) Help to run the show, after all your child **is** the lead?
   b) Turn up just in time to smile encouragingly?
   c) Play Candy Crush throughout the entire mind-numbingly boring hour, as your child will not join in anyway?

3) You have friends coming round for coffee. Are you:
   a) Looking forward to swapping some recipes and sharing your newly baked lemon drizzle cake?
   b) Quickly stuffing toys behind the sofa?
   c) Desperately trying to think of a believable group text to stop them all coming, as you cannot un-trash the house in time?

4) Your child is at an age where they ask lots of questions. Do you:
   a) Encourage them to ask more and excitedly book museum visits?
   b) Answer the best you can but sometimes feel frustrated?
   c) Find yourself thinking 'kill me now' quite a lot?

5) It is the school sports day are you:
   a) Standing at the finishing line, holding the tape, ready to photograph your child (naturally) winning?
   b) Standing chatting with the other parents, reluctantly keeping an eye out for your child's races?
   c) In a meeting at another school, about your other child's behaviour?

6) You need to leave for work are you:
   a) Wearing a crisp white blouse?
   b) Wearing a crisp white blouse with this morning's Weetabix on the front?
   c) Delayed at school due to 'an incident'?

7) You are planning a family day out. Are you:
   a) Looking forward to spending quality time with your family at a cultural event?
   b) Hoping it will go a bit better this time?
   c) Miserably resigned to suffering the consequences of such a stupid idea?

8) You are driving towards your house when you spot your neighbour. Do you:
   a) Beep excitedly, wave and invite them in for some newly baked cake?
   b) Smile and keep driving?
   c) Put your sunglasses on, look fixedly in the opposite direction and deliberately swerve a bit too close?

Results

Mostly A's: Perfect Parent - The 'Perfect Mother' (PM) descriptions throughout the book will apply to you. Whatever you think, no one really likes you.

Mostly B's: Good Parent: You are a 'Good Mother' in this book. You try your best but you are at risk of sliding into bad-tempered motherhood. This is however, preferable to aspiring to becoming a 'Perfect Mother'. At least you will have friends.

Mostly C's: Bad-Tempered Parent: Well done! You are a 'Bad-Tempered Mother' in this book. Very likely you are an aspiring Therapeutic Parent too. You will have lots of friends who are equally as bad-tempered and anti-social as you are. Most adopters and foster parents also fall into this category.....

....No? Just me then.

Characters

Bad-Tempered Mother

(AKA Therapeutic Parent)   Me

Rosie Rudey   Eldest daughter

Katie Careful   Second daughter

William Wobbly   Son

Sophie Spikey   2nd youngest daughter

Charley Chatty   Youngest daughter

LH   Lazy Husband (ex)

PH   Patient Husband (Ray)

PP   Patronising Professionals

AC   Arguing Children (group

                                name for all 5 children)

INP   Ignorant Non Parent

BMWC   Baking Mother with

                                Clipboard

GM   Good Mother

PM   Perfect Mother

IRT   Incredibly Rude Teenager

Disclaimer: None of the bad-tempered strategies and incidents described in this book are in any way recommended as good parenting practice or positive ways to interact with others. In fact they are often the opposite. They are, however, jolly good fun and will give you more free time.

PART ONE:

DEALING WITH ANNOYING PEOPLE

No slapping – Even for this….

Before I start, let's just get one thing clear. It's <u>NOT</u> ok to actually *slap* people who say:

1. But s/he looks so NORMAL!
2. Do you have any REAL children?
3. What happened to their REAL parents?
4. Why are they in care?
5. They should be grateful
6. Aren't you wonderful?/ You are doing an amazing job! (NB unless they are another adopter or foster parent and actually have a clue about what you are doing).
7. They will grow out of it
8. All children are like that/my (securely attached) children were just the same
9. Try using time out or a reward chart
10. They need a good slap
11. Can't you just send them back?
12. They won't remember anything
13. They should be settling down by now
14. I used to…..
15. In my time…
16. Just ignore them, they'll be fine
17. They are just attention seeking
18. You are too strict, lighten up a bit
19. Don't wish the time away
20. I bet you wish you had never 'taken them in'- (Like they were wandering about outside your house one night).

I have realised that it is not only the children that make us bad-tempered. It is other parents, other children, professionals and non-parents, who annoy us.

So.... people actually.

From rude shop assistants pretending they are deaf and blind, to pushy parents who we didn't invite, (and don't even like), 'popping in'.

Parents who decide to adopt or foster have the added irritations of dealing all too often, with clueless social workers and patronising birth parents extolling the virtues of Super Nanny and other nonsense behavioural strategies, which do not work with our children.

Some people are really good at hiding their bad-temperedness. They say annoying things like;

'He slept through the night from 3 days.'

'My children get on so well.'

'My teenager is so polite and helpful. I am really lucky.'

Well... whoopy-doo. Stop saying this. Really, just stop.

Now.

#1 Strategy – Repelling 'Baking-Mother-with-Clipboard'

Baking is at the very heart of 'normal' motherhood, something *our* mothers and grandmothers did. As an adopter of five Arguing Children, competing to lick the bowl out, 'baking' was not the nurturing, bonding experience I had hoped it would be. I felt that in order to be a 'Good Mother' I had to bake, preferably in a floury pinny, with Anchor butter in a packet, softening nearby.

The Bad-Tempered Mother (BTM) has a dilemma because she does not have the time, inclination or perhaps even the knowledge required, to carry out the 'baking' task. Baking-Mothers-With- Clipboards (BMWC) delight in using this lack of skill to taunt BTMs.

Annually I used to be approached at my children's school by BMWC. This is an exceptionally dangerous breed of 'Good Mother' as they have heightened sense of self-worth, often confused with 'smugbitchiness'. They also bully adopters and foster carers by smiling in a disdainful manner at them, and imply that they are superior in their parenting due to having given birth.

The BMWC had a tight little smug smile on her face as she bustled over to me. (You have to give BMWCs their due, as it is quite difficult to 'bustle' wearing jeans and T-shirt). Pen poised, BMWC asked me what she could 'put me down for', at the cake stall for the school summer fête next week.

As I fielded four children and two dogs with neat side swipes, and pointy-eyebrow-death-stares, I replied, "Hmm, let's see.... What help could you give me I wonder? I mean as a single parent with five children under 12, I could do with some free cakes."

I paused and looked at her clipboard meaningfully. There was a shocked silence. BMWC looked round nervously at other mothers for support. Other BTMs were smiling and winking happily at me, pretending not to listen, whilst Perfect Mothers shuffled about looking at the specks on their children's shiny-mirror shoes and swapping recipes.

BMWC started writing busily. I noticed her ears had gone quite red. She then muttered something about 'needing to speak to committee members' and left hurriedly.

The following year she (quite foolishly) approached me again and asked what cakes she could 'put me down for' to provide for the school 'bake in'. I said, "I don't know, I don't think I've bought any cakes this week."

She looked startled but smiled reassuringly at me and said that it wasn't a case of 'buying in' but *home baking*. I paused, gave her a long confused look and said, "Baking?!! No I don't do *that*. I am very busy with my *actual life*. I may have an old box of jam tarts I can send in though."

At this point she clearly remembered I was the incredibly rude, BTM from last year and beat a hasty retreat.

Strangely enough, my cooking talents were not called upon again. Although initially this was obviously hurtful, I tried to come to terms with it the best I could. If ever there was a need for genuine 'baking' to appear, ie at a family tea, I always found the local garden centre very handy.

#2 Strategy- Silencing Competitive Mothers

The 'Competitive Mother' (CM) usually places herself centrally at the school gate in order to ensure maximum audience when she announces (or casually slips into conversation) that little Natasha or Casper is now:

- Top in spellings
- Going to the grammar school
- Top in the Maths group
- Very kindly helping 'less able' children
- Part of a 'Specially Chosen Group' and in charge of an important project
- A black belt in Tai Kwon Do
- A grade 5 in ballet
- Attending pottery classes on Saturdays
- The proud owner of the area's first all organic children's garden
- Starting their own recycling project

This is very unfortunate for the BTM who finds herself struggling to remember what class her child is in - let alone what group she might be in for spelling. Exhausted by the bad behaviour, endless washing and ridiculous levels of arguing, the BTM sees school as 'respite for parents'.

When suddenly confronted with the boasting CM, urgent self-preservation action is called for. I say in a very loud voice (over the top of the boasting CM), "That's very interesting. My youngest actually didn't wet the bed last week, and do you know? My eldest has been accepted back into school after his last exclusion. We were so relieved because we really thought that was *it* this time, after he clocked the teacher one."

Pause to beam proudly at Competitive Mother.

This works really well. CM doesn't know if you are actually boasting or asking for parenting advice, so they tend to slope off.

The next time they start boasting, just clear your throat as if about to start talking. It's a good way of helping to remind them to shut their gobs.

Think of it as a kind of 'parent coaching'.

#3 Strategy: Avoiding School-gate Mummy Mafia

This one is easy-peasy. For a short time, I had to put all my children into a private school. (Argument with local education authority, long story- very common in adoption). Anyway, I discovered really quickly that the Mummy Mafia, driving the two inches from their house to the school in their 4x4s were interested in 4 things:

1) How much I was worth

2) My net contribution capacity for school fetes

3) Whether I was a possible 'husband stalker' (IE single parent).

4) What had happened to my children before they came to live with me.

After making the mistake of pausing politely to engage in conversation- and exiting the school playground feeling that I had been interrogated by the Third Reich-, the following day I took action.

I arrived at the school wearing a very fetching bright green and purple spotted 'pac-a-mac'. This was a left over from my army cadet camping days. I attracted several startled looks from 'the Yummies'. Some whispering and pointing ensued.

I then moved to stage 2 and pulled the voluminous plastic hood right down over my face. This meant I could only see my feet, and immediately avoided all eye contact with anyone. In this way I was able to move right through the throng of Mummy Mafia into the heart of 'child dump and run zone' with ease, and extract myself just as swiftly.

My pac-a-mac became a loyal friend. Unlike the Yummies.

4 Strategy: Managing Internet Shopping Delivery Drivers

The Bad-Tempered Mother likes Internet shopping because it is possible to look busy on the laptop and tell the Arguing Children (AC) that you are 'actually trying to make sure they can eat next week'. This can make the AC be quiet for a few minutes, as life without the prospect of Jammy Dodgers is a sobering thought indeed.

Meanwhile the BTM can frown meaningfully at the laptop and browse through her recent eBay purchases.

The only difficulty is that the BTM has to commit herself to actually being *in* the house for a two hour period. Invariably, towards the *end* of the two hour period, the phone will ring and the incredibly stupid delivery driver will tell you he is 'running late' or 'having problems finding you'.

The BTM knows that really, this means the driver knew two hours ago that there was no way he was going to get to you on time, but as you are a mother, and therefore have no life or purpose for living other than waiting in for shopping to arrive, he did not bother to ring earlier.

The mistake our driver had made, of course, was that he had erroneously assumed I was a Perfect Mother or at the very least a Good Mother. Imagine his dismay when he was confronted by me, the BTM.

On his arrival the grumpy Sainsbury's man moaned that we were 'hard to find'. This was a diversionary tactic. (Obviously he had children). He failed to realise that we were 'hard to find' because we needed to live in the middle of nowhere with 5 noisy, fairly destructive, absconding children, seven not very well trained dogs and two loudly bleating pygmy goats. I explained this to him and asked, "Would YOU like to be our neighbour?"

I then asked him why he had not bothered to read the comprehensive instructions I could clearly see on his clipboard, in big print, directing him to our house. I told him that if he was this late again, I was afraid he would have to let himself in and unpack the shopping. I made a big play of pretending to show him where the key was kept and tried to get him in the house to explain how I packed the freezer. He unloaded the shopping really quickly and left, looking anxiously over his shoulder.

#5 Strategy: Dealing with Unsolicited Parenting Advice

Don't worry, later in this chapter, there is a whole section dedicated to Patronising Professionals.

As I adopted *all* my children, I found birth parents were particularly keen to share their little 'pearls of wisdom' with me. I developed a thick skin very fast, hence my (fair) reputation for being rude, or bad-tempered.

It can be helpful to seek assistance from those offering their (unwanted) opinion at times of stress and arguments, as in these two examples:

Example 1- Interference from Perfect Mother

One morning, my Incredibly Rude Teenager (IRT), Katie Careful, screamed at me and told me I was, in fact a 'fat bitch'. Obviously I deserved this as I had had the audacity to ask her to close the door on her way out.

There then followed an explosive tantrum, mainly conducted before interested passersby, outside the house. One of the passersby was a middle-aged 'Perfect Mother' who unfortunately chose the time of maximum dysregulation to offer me her 'words of wisdom', an amused little self-righteous smug smile playing round her lips.

A Good or Perfect Mother would have been embarrassed but as a BTM I was so far past caring that I ran along the path, shouting threats at my IRT, whilst staring aggressively at the nosy passersby hoping they would phone Social Services to come and put her in a children's home.

I knew this was not a good therapeutic parenting strategy but I had officially 'lost it'.

Then with tilty head and crinkly eyes, the Perfect Mother said, "Oh dear someone's in a bad mood!" (Tinkly laugh), "Looks like someone needs a good talking to!"

Unfortunately, the PM had clearly mistaken me for a fellow PM having a bad day. She didn't realise she was dealing with a BTM. Taking a deep breath, I also put on my best PM crinkly eyed smile and bellowed, "WHAT a good idea! Why on earth didn't I think about SITTING MY CHILD DOWN AND TALKING TO HER INSTEAD OF CHASING HER UP THE ROAD IN DANGER OF SMACKING HER ROUND THE FACE?" Then, as if suddenly having the most brilliant idea, 'I know!! Why don't YOU take her home with you and have a nice little chat? It would help me out SO much. Just make sure you put all your valuables away…. Oh and hopefully you don't have any pets as that won't really be nice for them. Thank you SO much!!'

I then turned around and marched back into house for a well-deserved cup of tea, securely locking the door behind me. Looking through the window, I was gratified to see Katie and PM eyeing each other warily.

Example 2- Interference from Ignorant Non-Parent

Every BTM/ Therapeutic Parent keeps in her arsenal of weapons an Ignorant Non Parent. The INP is very useful because they have no idea about the relentless grind which makes previously good-tempered, INPs, transform into harassed bad-tempered parents, with sick on their shoulders and enormous bags, full of head-lice cream and wet wipes.

Sometimes, INPs say unhelpful things like;

- 'Hmm, you've changed since you've had children.'
- 'You're quite strict with your children aren't you?'
- 'Gosh, I never really realised what a big "shouting" voice you had before.'

At these times the BTM can have good fun putting on a (more) harassed expression and sighing loudly, possibly even forcing some pseudo tears into her eyes. The INP then naturally offers to have the kids for a couple of hours. After all, how difficult can it be?

The INP beams happily at the smiling children, excitedly anticipating the fun they are going to have. There are songs to sing, games to play, stories to read and cakes to bake. In fact, it will be quite difficult to fit all the exciting activities into a two hour slot.

The BTM skips quickly out of the door, clutching her credit card tightly to her chest, the nearest sofa with magazines and coffee is almost within her sights.

Even leaving fairly straightforward children with an INP is going to be a challenge. The INP will undoubtedly make fundamental errors such as 'giving in' and 'one more chocolate then'.

If you have been unkind enough to leave the INP with children with attachment problems, there is great fun to be had.

I once returned from one such excursion to find the INP (qualified nursery nurse) sitting in the middle of the bedroom floor crying. The children were literally swinging from the curtains, bouncing on the bed and dancing naked round the room. The INP looked at me and said, 'I'm *so* sorry.'

Earlier she had told me I was 'too strict' and needed to 'lighten up'. She thought she would give the children a treat by 'lightening up' and therefore confusing them with flexible boundaries, instantly catapulting them into a chaotic, power mad, frenzy of anarchic behaviour.

Funnily enough, she stopped offering advice afterwards.

#6 Strategy: Dealing with Receptionists

Dental Receptionist

Excerpt from diary entry 2006: *I took the children to the dentist today. Before I went I fantasised about the remote possibility that the dentist would somehow simultaneously anaesthetise all the children's tongues, thereby ceasing the arguing for up to three hours.*

At the dentist, the only thing that happened was that the receptionist got very cross with me for having so many children.

They did not easily fit into 'after school' appointments, she told me crossly.

I told her she should try fitting them into Tesco's for a weekly shop and invited her to join us afterwards.

She declined.

Medical Receptionist

The doctors' receptionist is a force to be reckoned with. What she doesn't know about major illnesses, life threatening diseases and any other heath issue is frankly not worth knowing.

If you should have the SHEER AUDACITY to phone the receptionist, asking for an actual doctor's appointment, be prepared for one of the following responses;

- Steely silence
- Death Stare down the phone
- Exasperating sighing
- Sulking
- Asking what the problem is, then repeating your name and symptoms in a loud voice to the crowded waiting room

As Therapeutic Parents have to deal with medical professionals on a regular basis to be entertained by the latest 'diagnosis argument', this receptionist is merely another obstacle to overcome. It is an unhappy marriage- that of medical receptionist and hypochondriac children.

The skilled BTM needs to take decisive action to deal with this particularly tricky breed of receptionist. Attack is definitely the best form of defence here.

Start the phone call with the most alarming claim you can think of. Forget anything behavioural. Gasping noises are good, and your Arguing Children may well oblige. Once you have her attention, wheeze that you need an urgent appointment. (Note; if she offers you a week next Tuesday, you have failed to convince her).

Once the receptionist reluctantly starts asking you about your child's (life threatening) symptoms, but immediately minimises them to 'So she has a mild cold then?' etc.-ask her what her medical qualifications are. Go on to state that your child was misdiagnosed last year and that you have just won substantial damages for her. Then ask for her full name and job title. This normally does the trick.

I have not included advice here about getting a doctor's appointment for yourself, as we all know that Therapeutic Parents never have the time for such trivia.

School Receptionists

This is a challenging receptionist to deal with. Naturally the school receptionist's job is to get the maximum number of children sent home for vacuous reasons, leaving the school unfettered by them, messing the place up and taking up her time.

For this reason, in recent years it has practically become illegal to put a plaster on a child, give them any form of medication, or even offer a comforting hug at school.

NO, *far* better to phone up Mum or Dad, drag them out of their important deal-breaking meeting 50 miles away, (or more likely a meeting about 'behaviour' in an adjacent school), only to find when arriving at the school that child is 'better' now and no longer requires the tiny medication, which appeared to be the only way to save their life a mere 30 minutes earlier.

I learnt to take a hard line really fast, and I know that as a BTM I carved out an enviable reputation for myself, making sure most school receptionists avoided phoning me if at all possible.

On one occasion, the school receptionist phoned me to say one of my daughters had 'been sick'. My natural BTM response was, "How do you know? Did you actually SEE the sick?"

Stunned silence.

Obviously it transpired my daughter had NOT been sick but for a brief moment I won the 'Nastiest Mother' award from the school.

Similarly, on another occasion, I was summoned to go to collect Rosie Rudey who had 'fallen over in the corridor' leaving her 'unable to walk'. Now as a Therapeutic Parent *and* BTM of children with attachment disorder I was fairly confident that this was also a lie. I was very cross at having to go up to the school for the 8th time that week.

As I strode across the playground, the school receptionist appeared, wheeling my daughter in an *actual wheelchair*. Like a fishwife, I screamed across the playground, "Get out of that chair and walk RIGHT NOW!"

To the receptionist's utter amazement, my daughter did exactly that. I could practically hear her thinking "It's a miracle!" and recounting this in the staff room later on.

Some minutes later I phoned the school receptionist to inform her that my daughter's broken leg had now healed so well that she was playing hop scotch in the back garden.

I then gave her a free phone-based training session lasting approximately 30 minutes about how to handle this kind of event in the future, and why she must NEVER phone me again without being 100% sure she had not been taken in.

Once I was satisfied I had used up the same amount of her time, as she had used of mine, I ended the call. This is called 'natural consequences'.

Another really easy way of dealing with ill-judged fake 'emergency' calls from the school is to simply be unavailable. So the school receptionist phones up and says, 'Can you come and pick up William, as he *says* he has a tummy ache?'

Me (disingenuously): "Oh dear! Oh no! Poor little boy. Unfortunately, I am 60 miles away …."

a) Visiting my relative in hospital,

b) At important conference,

c) Having urgent medical procedure, (delete as appropriate).

"Don't worry though I will leave right now. Traffic was bad on M5 but I should be there in 3 hours." (IE 5 minutes before school kicking out time). Receptionist then says not to worry, and yet another miracle occurs as William makes an astounding recovery in time to eat a hefty lunch.

#7 Strategy: Dealing with Shop Assistants

BTMs are often quite impatient. This is because they always have a large number of jobs to achieve in a small amount of time. When they go into a shop to buy, say a phone, it is not because they are having a lovely shopping experience and are considering the pros and cons of a variety of phones for their AC's Christmas presents.

Unlike Good Mothers who begin shopping for Christmas in the January sales, BTMs only go shopping for most goods because there is an urgent need.

This need may arise from an Incredibly Rude Teenager smashing a smaller Arguing Child's phone on the bedroom wall, or it may arise from the BTM's pressing requirement to buy loud speakers so she can create a zone within the house, where she can play 'Hits from the 80s' at top volume to drown out the arguing and screaming noises.

Either way, the BTM, on entering the shop, immediately identifies the make and model of the phone/ DVD player/ speakers she requires, and proceeds to purchase within approximately 2 minutes. At this stage of the transaction, the BTM does not need to be told by the gifted 12 year old sales assistant, that, 'that model is our last one and is only for display.'

The best action to take in this situation is as follows:

1) Assume every item you ever want to buy is 'the last one' or 'display only'

2) Start your enquiry to purchase with, 'I am only buying the phone/DVD/speakers if I can have it today, put it in my car and drive it away forthwith.' This immediately identifies you to the shop assistant as a BTM. He is unlikely to mess with you as you remind him of his mum.

3) Start unplugging the security wires straight away and pretend you can't hear his protestations above the sirens.

4) Pick up the item and say firmly that you do not require the box.

5) Proceed to till.

The 'following shop assistant' simultaneously and annoyingly asks if they can 'help you' or if you 'found everything you're looking for' whilst stalking you. Although easily ignored the BTM can find herself rushing quickly around the aisles, desperately trying to out-run the stalking shop assistant. Interestingly, I found that I was approached much less when I had my five Arguing Children with me.

When shopping alone though… Oh the joy! I could easily, simply leave the shop as soon as the assistant moved towards me. This is only effective if you use the same shop regularly. The assistant soon learns to leave you well alone and you can continue in peace.

If there is one thing worse than the shop assistant who constantly follows you around, it is the one who wilfully ignores you.

The BTM is expert in dealing with this particular species, as they remind her of her Incredibly Rude Teenagers.

When the BTM is waiting at the till to purchase her hurriedly selected items, the teenage shop assistants invariably stand in a little group discussing the latest eyebrow pencil colours, how drunk they got at the weekend, and whether or not their manager is a bitch today. They treat the BTM's presence as if an annoyingly rude person is trying to barge into their private conversation.

I have found over the years that the very best solution is to simply start singing loudly. I even have a favourite song the words go like this;

"Invisible I feel like I'm invisible, you treat me like I'm not really there and you don't even care I know this romance it ain't going nowhere."

(Alison Moyet)

Amazingly this seems to do the trick and there is a hurried movement to serve me (albeit with much sulking and sighing), to ensure that I stop singing immediately.

I can't think why... The Arguing Children seemed to have similar reactions.

#8 Strategy: Dealing with Pushy Parents

Oh my life! Save me from the Pushy Parent who insists on coming to my house, foisting her revolting children on me and sitting in MY armchair consuming cups of tea for hours on end, blatantly STEALING my precious time. I don't like you, I have never liked you, and I have never invited you. Stop coming to my house.

That is what is going through my head.

The BTM has to find a way to actually make it clear to the Pushy Parent that they are not invited. Often, the Pushy Parent is confused with the Baking-Mother-With-Clipboard. The difference being that the Pushy Parent is obviously not 'baking' because she is too busy going to other people's houses, eating *their* cakes.

The BTM may actually have electric gates installed so that nobody can come up to their front door and ring the bell without getting through the gates first. This is inspired brilliance because it means the BTM can look out the window, see who it is, and make a decision as to whether or not she is going to open the gates to the drive. She doesn't even have to *speak* to them!

If you cannot afford electric gates, or your property does not allow it, you can choose one of the following three options;

1) Pretend you are deaf and smile inanely when she starts telling you she is coming round.

2) Make sure you're out when she comes and then simply say you forgot she was coming. Repeat as necessary.

3) Look her straight in the eyes and say, 'No I am too busy.'

If you're very bad-tempered, or very brave you can say, "No I am too busy and we not really friends are we anyway?" Tinkly laugh.

The best strategy to use to avoid these people, is to go to work. Even if you're not at work- pretend to be at work. You can tell everyone you are working from home. This deals with most Pushy Parents. If they are stupid enough to try to trick you by 'popping in' they will have to leave immediately because you can answer the door holding your laptop, phone at ear, and harassed expression.

#9 Strategy: Nuking Nosy People

When you adopt or foster a child, Nosy People want to know

- What happened to your children

- Why they are with you,

- What happened to their birth parents

Luckily as a BTM I was able to deal with this very effectively. I would give the Nosy Person a 'Paddington Hard Stare' and ask, "So, how *is* your sex life at present?"

In the shocked silence that followed, I would say, "In terms of personal questions, the one I just asked you is comparable to the one you asked me."

Smile and withdraw.

#10 Repelling Neighbours (and other people who 'pop in')

The BTM is very good at spotting lurkers. Lurkers are normally neighbours who loiter about outside the gate, waiting to pop in on any pretext whatsoever. Sometimes there is pseudo 'hedge clipping' or 'looking for the postman' associated behaviour.

Although it is possible to deal with these people in a similar way to the way we deal with Pushy Parents, we have to remember that we might need them to phone the emergency services during our next child related incident. We also do *not* want them to phone the police every time our Arguing Children have an outdoor tantrum. Therefore, the BTM has to be a little bit more careful when it comes to managing the unwelcome neighbour.

My preferred method of dealing with them is to make sure they understand I am 'very busy indeed'. Invitations to join in the local 'Open Gardens' or 'Neighbourhood Watch' are met with wistful smiles, and busy watch glances of 'If only I could.'

If they do manage to get in your garden or (horror) in your house, then ensure that you have lots of barking dogs and noisy children flinging their arms around the unsuspecting neighbour's legs.

If you are lucky enough to have children with attachment disorder, it is likely that the children will ask the neighbour to be their new mummy or daddy. Beam benevolently if this happens, then smile sadly at them and ask them for some help. Unless you are very unfortunate indeed they will quickly withdraw and be reluctant to visit you again.

When neighbours invite you to coffee mornings simply forget to go. (See Part 4: Annoying Thing #7 Coffee mornings and small-talk).

Another tactic is 'swift exiting'. When my neighbour came round to try to give me information about dull changes to our street signs, she wanted to talk to me for about half an hour. It was very easy to simply walk straight out of the front door holding my car keys, greeting the Parish Councillor with a cry of regretful surprise. "Oh I was just going out I didn't realise you were there!"

This way you can continue getting into your car, anxiously checking the time and taking a pretend phone call while she forces the magazine into your hand.

Drive away waving apologetically.

#11 Dispatching Ex-Partners Effectively.

As a self-confessed BTM I had to deal very quickly and swiftly with ex partners. This makes it sound like there were loads but actually there was only one, (the AC acting as a natural partner deterrent for many years), who needed actual encouragement to leave.

He was very annoying indeed and had caused us all some grief and upset. What he failed to grasp was that I would be absolutely thrilled if he left me for another woman, and I tried without success to match him up with hapless less deserving 'friends'. After I had been trying to get rid of him for two years I needed to act decisively.

Being a busy might-as-well-be- single parent, it needed to be something requiring minimum effort. It seemed a good idea to list him on eBay as a 'Broken Action Man'. I added photos and a description saying he 'had not worked for some years' and that he was to all intents and purposes 'useless'. I then explained that no returns would be accepted and started the bidding at 1p. I was very pleased to sell him quickly within three days on a 'buyer collects basis' for 3p.

Yes, this *is* a true story.

#12 Managing Other People's Irritating Children

If there is one thing that gets on the BTM's nerves more than anything else, it is other people's badly behaved children invading her personal space. This is especially annoying when one has managed to dispatch one's own Arguing Children for a brief period of much needed silence, sometimes called 'respite'.

Wherever I tried to grab those few precious minutes, the badly behaved screaming toddler who enjoys throwing toys at his parents, (and anyone else in the vicinity), will be found smiling snottily at me from a proximity of about 6 inches, whenever I am:

- In the quiet corner of the airport departure lounge,

- In the 'grown up' restaurant (Ie not Pizza Hut)

- In the doctor's surgery waiting room

- On the upgraded part of the plane, (particularly annoying, it should *not* be allowed)

- In the 'adults only' pool

Huffing and sighing is not effective when dealing with this particular problem. This is because the irritating children invariably belong to Perfect Mothers. There is a direct correlation between the amount of perfection aspiration in the mother and the capacity to irritate in the child.

BTMs know that their own children are annoying to everybody, including themselves. Perfect Mothers think that their children are amusing little darlings who everyone will smile at indulgently, because they are 'oh so funny, sweet and amusing.'

It is our job as BTMs to educate the Perfect Mothers into understanding how irritating their little dears are, and why they need to remove them from the 'BTM danger zone' immediately. There are two methods to dispatch them efficiently;

1) Professional Standard Death Stare. By fixing the snotty-nosed, exasperating child with my steely death-stare, the child quickly makes a tactical withdrawal. Their PM might look at me suspiciously but by then I am reading my magazine and appear to be unaware of my surroundings.

2) Loud sneezing and hacking coughing in general direction of child. This results in the PM quickly recalling the child and disinfecting it.

3) Allowing own Arguing Children free reign if they are available. It might be handy to talk about 'surprises' or bring in an element of uncertainty. This is sure to increase arguing and violence.

Even more tortuous are all the parents who keep their children up late on holiday, toiling under the delusion that all the other holidaymakers will find their children just as hilarious and wonderful as they do.

Obviously the main reason they do this is selfishness. Even though the cruise ship/ hotel/ holiday park etc. may offer a wall-to-wall babysitting service this is not good enough for the Perfect Parents who need to have their children welded to their side at all times.

The end result is a small group of parents drinking alcohol and enjoying themselves while the child sits staring at Peppa Pig on the iPad, bleary eyed with tiredness. At some point the bleary eyed tiredness becomes 'naughty' behaviour as the child selfishly demands attention and the need for sleep. The child is then told off by the embarrassed (half cut) not-so-Perfect-now Parent.

Faced with this situation several nights in a row, I found myself exclaiming, (in loud tones), "That child is clearly tired and needs to go to bed. Poor child!" etc. Patient Husband tried in vain to drag me away.

It wasn't a pleasant end to the night.

#13 Dealing with Extended Family

The list at the beginning of this chapter gives a good overview of all the irritating, patronising things which are said to Therapeutic Parents, making them much more bad-tempered.

Naturally, extended family also believe that they are _the_ parenting experts, regardless of whether or not they have any children. Even worse, because they are family, they do not have any social inhibitors to prevent the fountain of ill-informed condescension gushing forth.

Adopters have the added bonus of helpful statements from friends and family like, "Why don't you send them back?" or, the ever unpopular, "You'd think they'd be grateful!"

Those with securely attached birth children are particularly exasperating for BTM's who are Therapeutic Parents.

Most BTMs do not _have_ in-laws on account of the fact that their husbands or partners have already left them because they are so grumpy. If, however, you are unfortunate enough to have in-laws who do everything in their power to annoy or undermine you then the following action is called for.

- Give them a copy of an extremely complex parenting book. Tell them this is the model you are following, and unless they stick to it rigidly they cannot visit.

- Invite them regularly for Sunday dinner but make sure that the dinner is inedible. Give yourself a different version of the dinner which _is_ edible and exclaim how lovely it is all the way through the meal, encouraging them to 'eat up,' while smiling brightly. This at least stops them coming round for meals in the future.

- Put your Arguing Children together with the annoying in-laws and then exit the building for a minimum of three hours.

Switch phone to silent, or better still, leave it obviously behind.

My adult children have subsequently gone on to have children themselves and now, one of the main things they complain about during pregnancy is how annoying it is when people home in on 'The Bump'. They describe older females ceasing to make eye contact with them, staring at their stomach and rushing towards them to grab it like it's some kind of tasty, doughy chocolate cake, requiring a quick knead.

I helpfully bought my daughters a T-shirt saying, 'Hands off,' but even this was not enough for the most determined of stomach grabbers.

My daughters have in their turn become Bad-Tempered Mothers, and this began during the pregnancy whilst repelling the stomach grabbers.

"Why oh why," they used to ask me, "Do people only see me now as a baby oven, cooking their new grandchild/ niece/nephew/ playmate?"

I could not answer as I was <u>not</u> (and never have been) in the stomach-grabber camp. I merely offered them the following effective early BTM strategies, designed to repel the most determined of stomach grabbers;

- Pretend to go into labour every time they touch you. Extreme but effective.

- Wear a pretend TENS machine which actually gives the grabber an electric shock

- When they walk in and stare at your stomach, quickly lie on the floor or sofa to establish eye contact, wave frantically and say, "Cooey! I'm here!"

- Simply give them a Paddington Hard Stare as they descend and say in deathly tone, "Do not touch me."

The last one is my favourite. Sets the tone for the future when you need to say, 'Do NOT give him chocolate.'

It is just as trying when you adopt or foster. Members of the extended family seem to think that the child is a new prize exhibit and complain loudly that you are not willing to parade your traumatised child around the country, introducing them to yet another raft of strangers.

How unreasonable and bad-tempered of you. And lazy probably.

#14 Managing Tedious Birthing Boasters

As I adopted all my children I was 'unlucky' enough to miss the torture and pain of pregnancy and childbirth. This meant I was also unable to join in the excruciating blow-by-blow account of 'The Birthing Experience/Trauma/Joy' (delete as appropriate), that the Tedious Birthing Boasters in my vicinity seemed to enjoy recounting loudly at every opportunity. All appeared to be having a little competition about how their birth was worse/ easier/ than everyone else's.

I used to take great delight in modestly stating that I had five children but had 'still managed to keep my figure.' This was clearly a blatant lie, as I had naturally ballooned to the size of a small independent country whilst on my post-adoption-cake-&-chocolate-comfort-eating diet.

The Tedious Birthing Boasters did not know how to reply, as they knew my children were adopted, but instantly worried that no one else knew, so felt unable to challenge me. The birth boasting tailed off quite dramatically as people remembered I might be excluded.

Bit awkward. (For them).

#15 Neutralising ~~Wise and~~ Patronising Professionals

Every parent, bad-tempered or otherwise, has to deal with Patronising Professionals. As an adopter I thought it was just us facing a plethora of 'experts', all of whom knew better than we did. But no! When my daughter had her baby I discovered a whole new raft of Patronising Professionals, cunningly disguised as helpful health visitors and midwives.

The thing is though, as 'One Who Had Given Birth' there was a natural pecking order. Her child was definitely *her* child. So whilst there was fun to be had by the Patronising Professionals giving her conflicting advice and frightening her half to death during the first few weeks, there was never any real fear that she would 'burp him' the wrong way, and find him taken into care immediately.

Therapeutic Parents have no such security. They often find themselves patronised and undermined at every turn, with casual allusions to moving children, or other undermining and sometimes threatening 'support strategies' squatting malignantly nearby, in silent threat.

Patronising Professional (1) Social Workers

Now, I do speak as an ex social worker and have to take my fair share of the blame. I apologise here, unreservedly for all the ridiculous suggestions I made to my foster parents about the best ways to parent their foster child.

Yes, you were right. Sorry I had absolutely no idea what I was talking about. You see they didn't train us for that at Uni. I knew all about the Children Act and Freud, but I didn't know how to give proper strategies to people looking after children who had been through trauma. So, I fell back on my Super Nanny methods and advised time out, naughty step and reward charts galore! I didn't listen or care when you protested that these methods 'didn't work.'

'Pah!' I thought, 'she is just being negative. I know this all works.'

And so began my vertical learning-curve climb into the world of adoptive parenting. During the ascent I learnt the hard way that the foster parents had been right all along. Those old fashioned methods did not work with my children. The standard methods were meant for standard parents, climbing a standard steep hill. I, on the other hand, was climbing an ice cliff wearing a blindfold.

What I NEEDED as a mother of five children with attachment disorder, was a Wise *un-Patronising* Professional, to come along and offer me a variety of ice picks and crampons, along with some nice warm clothing and chocolate for nurture and warmth. What did I get instead? Patronising Professionals, unhelpfully offering me roller-skates to wear, and heavy bags to carry during my climb, whilst unsupportively standing by and criticising my climbing method.

As I became more bad-tempered and frustrated, a creeping sense of shame reminded me, in a taunting little smug voice, about all the people I had given roller-skates to over the years.

In order to pay them back (in the Karmic way), I obviously had to suffer. Over the next 15 years, I received several pairs of roller-skates at key 'sliding down the mountain' moments when social workers:

- Told me repeatedly that my children would 'grow out of it'. (Sadly attachment disorder can be 'grown out of' in the same way that you can grow out of having ginger hair).

- Wrote an assessment 14 pages long, which basically said they didn't know what to do, but whatever happened it was my fault.

- Approved me for 5 children, changed their minds and placed 3, changed their minds a year later and asked me to have the older 2, placed the older 2, tried to change their minds again and remove them. (Naturally as a BTM they had a fight on their hands and failed).

- Told me my son 'would not remember anything' so therefore all his behaviours were down to my parenting.

- Did not notice when I had a stroke mid conversation, and continued filling out a form and asking me questions. (She said afterwards that she thought I had been 'a bit quiet').

There are many more examples but they are too depressing to list. I quickly learnt some brilliant ways of neutralising social workers who attempted to patronise me.

1) Remind them I too was a social worker, (partially effective).

2) Remind them I ran an 'Ofsted 'Outstanding' therapeutic fostering agency, (temporary kudos and respite from social worker rudeness, whilst frantic background checking and attempts to dismiss new information occurred).

3) Give them one of the many books from my bookshelf about therapeutic parenting and refuse to speak to them till they had read it.

4) Smile sweetly and say with a sad face, "Oh what a shame! They didn't teach you about attachment at Uni either did they? Never mind. What would you like to know?"

In my training courses, I advise parents to use a combination of 3 & 4.

Many parents we work with have now tried this and also used my book 'Therapeutic Parenting in a Nutshell' to good effect. (I have had to tell a few parents that they can't use the book to whack people round the head with it though).

Violence is not the way forward.

In the interests of fairness, I have to add that I have met some truly brilliant and inspiring social workers. I have had the pleasure of working with a fair few over the years and I can honestly say that I would not have developed the insight I (finally) managed to find, without the very skilled support of one or two excellent social workers. A good social worker, skilled in compassionate, meaningful support, with a strong foundation in childhood trauma, really does make all the difference.

That will be £50 please.

Patronising Professional (2) Teachers

Over the years, well-meaning teachers have said the following to me:
1) He looks so normal.
2) Would you like us to supply you with a guide as to what should be in his lunch box? (He ate nearly everything on the way to school).
3) He will be FINE! Stop worrying! – (Going on school trip to dark caves, - he was NOT fine. Cue more trauma nightmares for following 6 weeks).
4) He has to fit in with the other children, we have to treat them all the same.
5) He won't fit in with the other children.

One of the key stress times is when the teacher announces that we are looking at 'families' as the next topic. No matter how many times we explained my children did not have any baby photos, the teachers continued to consider me as someone who was just 'being difficult'.

Now obviously as a BTM I *was* being difficult quite a lot of the time, but in this particular instance I was not.

When I reminded the teacher yet again that my child did not have baby photos, she said, "Oh well just bring any old one in. He won't know."

The best way to deal with this kind of ignorance is Pointy-Eyebrow-Death-Stare mixed with Steely Silence. This is really effective as the teacher starts frantically going back over the last bit of the conversation and invariably modifies her initial statement. This strategy can also be used to good effect with the "Would you like our nutrition guide for his packed lunch?" question.

I took great exception to letters from school explaining to me how to make a packed lunch for my child. (I have written a whole section later on regarding packed lunches and a separate section on 'letters home').

I went to the school with said letter, read it out to the Headmistress in a patronising voice and asked her if she would like me to come in and explain her job to her.

She didn't.

Dealing with School Reward Charts

Schools are often very fixated on traditional methods of behavioural management, although some schools in the U.K. are now thankfully moving away from reward charts and other outdated behaviour modification methods.

I once had a teacher call me in to speak to me with a disappointed-teacher-face about how saddened she was that my daughter was always at the bottom of the reward chart and seemed to enjoy being there, 'no matter what rewards were offered.'

I told the teacher that I offered training for schools working with children who had suffered trauma. I asked her if she would like me to show her how to simply modify the reward chart in order to make it more effective.

The teacher was thrilled and willingly agreed. I marched over to the reward chart, pulled it off the wall, threw it on the floor, stamped on it several times, then picked it up again and ripped it into several pieces.

The teacher sat looking on in open-mouthed horror. "There you go!" I exclaimed happily, "It will work perfectly now!"

I may have been in compassion fatigue at the time.

We mutually decided it might be best to move schools shortly afterwards. So I moved counties after having found a school which did not do 'reward charts'. Believe me it was worth the upheaval.

(For 'Not Doing Homework' See Minimising Drudgery #15)

Patronising Professional (3) Therapists/ Counsellors

Therapists are a special brand of PP as they have a lot of intimidating, important letters after their names. Sometimes these letters are meaningful and helpful to Therapeutic Parents. Letters like DDP (Dyadic Developmental Psychotherapy), or even the magic phrase, 'attachment therapist' and an allusion to even being an adopter!

Usually the letters and words are unhelpful and are something like 'British Academy of Psychotherapeutic Important Person, with a good working knowledge of what a secure attachment looks like, skilled in shifting blame and dishing out a bit of judgement'.

The best therapy always took place where I was present and could put in gentle reality check reminders, keeping everyone grounded. ("No darling, remember we don't have a blender so could not have put the puppy in it.") This was *so* important and helped my children to separate past trauma from 'life today'.

Skilled therapy and intervention has its place of course, and the right therapy which *includes* the Therapeutic Parent on some level, is invaluable and powerful. *(See Therapeutic Parenting in a Nutshell,)*

The enthusiastic 'School Counsellor' is guaranteed to strike dread into the heart of any Therapeutic Parent, who knows that this is the equivalent of giving a master manipulator free reign with an unsuspecting 3-year-old. The 'master manipulator' being their child of course.

The *unskilled* therapist/counsellor, will derive satisfaction and professional fulfilment from our children's frank and full, teary- eyed disclosures. They appear largely unaware that the child is usually merely operating in survival mode, and ensuring they keep 'the sympathetic face' fully engaged with them for as long as possible. There may even be sweet rewards if the therapist is particularly uneducated.

A Counsellor's unwillingness or inability to share facts with the parent leads to all kinds of interesting situations.

On one memorable occasion, William was 15 and was enjoying a fair bit of attention from PPs through absconding and pretend-risk-taking. (I didn't think it was risky watching his friend's TV and eating sandwiches, but what do I know)? Apparently it was a 'cause for concern' so he was allocated a very wise Counsellor (PP) through the school.

William had clearly had a lovely time enthralling the Counsellor with his exciting and traumatic stories which elicited rewards in the form of jelly babies and trips out. They also handily excused him from lessons on several occasions. Especially Maths. We noticed a strong propensity for urgent 'counselling sessions' during those times. (Later on Charley needed to 'urgently see' the School Counsellor when it was time for P.E).

At a multi-agency meeting (called by me), the Counsellor put on his 'disappointed face' to inform the whole meeting that William had 'only stolen money because he needed batteries for his torch, as there was no electricity in his room'.

I knew that William had stolen money to go to the amusement arcade with his friends, as he had told me the previous day so I paused momentarily to reflect on his emerging creative skills. I imagined the Counsellor using his best 'sympathetic face' and briefly felt sorry for him. This did not last long as obviously there was a sea of accusatory faces waiting for me to explain why I neglected my teenage son in such a way. The BTM part of me rose up angrily in defence.

I informed him that not only did William own 'nothing at all with batteries,' (due to the fact that he ate them), but also that he had a wind up torch. I asked how realistic he thought this story was and enquired about his experience with children with attachment difficulties.

The flustered Counsellor quickly used the old 'We have to believe the child,' reliable go-to all-encapsulating-blame-shifting-statement, with a triumphant flourish. This was greeted with satisfied nods and a sense of relief that the other PPs in the meeting were now on safer ground.

BTM in full flow, I then completely ruined his Victory Speech by giving a lengthy explanation about attachment, trauma and false allegations, then invited anyone less keen to join in a blame fest, to decamp to our home a few minutes walk away, to satisfy themselves that William's room did indeed have electricity.

I then thanked everyone for their time and said I thought we might possibly manage better as a family if they all just went away and wrote reports somewhere else.

The meeting ended shortly afterwards and PH and I continued trying to mend William alone. On the whole this was more successful.

Other unhelpful 'therapeutic interventions with the children included:

- In family therapy – therapist continually referring to anger and 'full bottles of milk' being in danger of spilling. This led to the children having little bets about how far into the session it would be before the inevitable 'bottle of milk' was mentioned. Resulting in much eye catching and loud guffaws of undermining laughter, (including from me). Culminating in Rosie Rudey stating, "If you patronise me once more with 'bottles of milk', I will punch you."

- In one to one Psychotherapy with Katie – Therapist recommended that the answer to ALL her attachment problems was to spend time with horses. I informed her that she already went riding, so she suggested we 'bought a horse'. As we strongly suspected Katie of 'helping' the hamster to find its way to the magical hamster kingdom, we did not think this was the answer. I asked the Therapist if she had read Dan Hughes at all. Needless to say there was a blank stare.

- An eminent (thankfully now retired) Child Psychiatrist wrote *(in a report) - As Sophie was removed (from extreme neglect and abuse) at the age of 18 months she will have no conscious memory of her early life and is unlikely to have any long term difficulties.*

Well try telling my children that. Obviously they did not listen....

PART TWO:

MINIMISING DRUDGERY

We know, once we get to a 'training course' (AKA free lunch and offloading opportunity), with other exhausted Therapeutic Parent friends, the truth will out. We share stories in hushed-Patronising-Professional-avoidance tones, about our arguing, ungrateful children, and our Incredibly Rude Teenagers, but we airbrush out the day to day crushing grind of recycling, school runs, and nonsense questions. There isn't time to talk about normal parenting irritations and drudgery.

As my adult children had their own birth children, I also witnessed first-hand the bleary-eyed stunned expressions of parents catapulted from cosy, lie in twosome-ness, into a sick spattered waking-night war zone.

I have come to the conclusion that it is the 'parenthood lie' which forces us all into this post adoption/birth zombie zone, which is almost a state of post-traumatic stress disorder in itself! I am just as guilty of maintaining this lie, although I tried *so* hard to tell them!

When Rosie (no longer Rudey) was pregnant, she asked me to tell her 'honestly' what her experience as a mother might be. I replied, "Well I would say it's;

- 50% crushing boredom, tempered only by a morbid interest in how the day will be survived with unprecedented levels of sleep deprivation.

- 30% poo, sick, wee, snot, bogeys and spots with assorted childhood illnesses.

- 10% planning lovely family outings and events.

- 5% having a horrible time at the planned family outing.

- 5% having a lovely time, taking pictures of said lovely time, in order to be able to pretend later that that was indeed the majority of the childhood experience."

Rosie looked at me, wide eyed and horrified.

"Only kidding!" I said quickly.

This is how the lie is perpetuated. This is why she is now becoming a BTM in training.

#1 Rejecting Drudgery

As a BTM I quickly found ways to minimise the drudgery of parenthood and allow myself more time to sip wine, contemplate the world and generally misbehave. I know that many of my methods were frowned upon by the Perfect Mothers around me, but did I care? No not very much. I did not care when I skipped happily down the road with my shop bought picnic. I did not even care when I sunbathed on holiday with earphones in so I could not hear the children hitting each other in the swimming pool. I did not care when my children went to school in un-matching socks.

But I did have a lot more free time.

#2 Vehicle Breakdown = Spa Day

To most people, breaking down on the side of a busy motorway in the middle of the day is a not an ideal situation. If you are a Therapeutic Parent and you break down WITHOUT CHILDREN in the car, this is our equivalent of a spa day.

When I got a flat tyre on the M5 I had to wait for an hour for the breakdown recovery truck. Ok it was a bit noisy and I did have to sit behind a crash barrier but - OH! It was lovely! I had time to post a few selfies on Facebook, play Candy Crush and catch up with my emails.

No one was whining or moaning. No one bothered phoning me for favours and no one was surprised that I hadn't made dinner or attended another pointless meeting to explain the word 'attachment' to the school.

I commented on our Therapeutic Parents' Facebook page that I was enjoying my breakdown experience. I was immediately inundated with responses, (it was our second most popular post ever) with fond reminiscences of blissful hours spent in hospital waiting rooms, dental surgeries, and (my favourite) a whole hour in an MRI scanner listening to music.

Well we have to take our breaks however we can.

#3 Avoiding Recycling and 'Greenness'

Perfect Mothers patiently recycle everything and sing happily to themselves while they do it. Competitive Mothers recycle the most and also 'upcycle' prolifically and then tell everyone all about it. Bad-Tempered Mothers don't recycle at all, or only pretend to. Generally, they don't believe in global warning as;

- It is too time consuming to have to do so,

- It just creates another job

- It is nothing compared to the surrounding war zone, laughingly referred to as 'home'.

- Patient Husband does not seem very keen on sorting out the cereal boxes from the loo roll interiors for some reason.

BTMs have far too much to do peeling sick off the wallpaper. Some are heard to mutter, "If the government want me to wash their bloody tins before they put them in the bin, then they can bloody well come round here and wash them themselves."

#4 Dealing with Dog Poo

When out walking dogs it is expected to pick up the poo in order to protect our spaces. This can be an onerous task for BTMs with several children and dogs in tow.

Astoundingly, BTMs have been known to put an old brown glove in a dog poo bag. It is believed that this is done for the sole purpose of pretending to pick up the dog poo on a particularly busy morning. No one in their right mind would demand to check the contents of the 'glove in poo bag', so the BTM can safely walk the dogs, with impunity, self-righteously swinging the pseudo poo filled bag, without actually having to stop and pick poo up.

I don't actually know anyone who did this. I have just heard about it.

Apparently, (I am told) even GMs tend to bend down near the poo and pluck blades of grass. They then walk purposefully to the poo bin. It is only PMs who actually pick up the poo. Smiling happily to themselves, neatly clipped, newly de pooed poodle frolicking nearby with dungaree-d blond children vying to help.

Or they do not need to pick up poo at all as their Au Pair does it.

#5 Surviving School Plays and Performances

School plays are a huge trial for BTMs. Firstly, you have to come to terms with the knowledge that only Competitive Mothers' children ever play 'Mary' or 'The Prince'. My children were 'additional sheep' or 'extra star', or on one memorable occasion '3rd bush'.

I am sure CMs enjoy their children's school plays. They obviously get there first, sometimes using pretexts like 'setting out chairs' or 'helping' in order to ensure they have front row seats so they can smarm about and simper.

As a BTM, I did initially try to appear enthusiastic at my children's school plays. I pretended not to mind when my 5-year-old 'additional angel' refused to sing, or engage in *any* way in a single song.

In a scenario familiar to most Therapeutic Parents, similarly, another year, I pretended I found it amusing when my 5-year-old could be heard screaming loudly from the vestry, insisting she was wearing her pink sparkly shoes with her angel costume.

All the other sweet little 5-year-old angels filed in dressed appropriately and behaving in an angel-like manner, hands folded neatly in front of them, in suitable 'angel praying' mode. After some delay, the teacher carried out a red, fat lumpen child in a white dress. The red, fat lumpen-one was extremely angry and attempting to punch the other angels. PMs and Good Mothers looked around in an amused, smug way, trying to identify the poor unfortunate mother of the red, fat lump. I assumed PM pose and also looked around, smiling and nodding in a benign, curious manner.

After this I found school plays more and more of a trial. It was not helped by the fact that my children's infant school thought it was a great idea to have the same play, year in and year out. This meant I had to sit through the same damn play 5 times.

Now, I always take some form of entertainment with me. I recommend this to every BTM. Larger newspapers are a bit conspicuous so try to avoid those.

I find it useful to slip in last and get a really dreadful seat, that way there is usually nobody sitting next to you. My favourite spot is behind the church pillar. From there I can safely make eye contact with whoever is playing 'additional sheep' and wave enthusiastically, like I am really looking forward to watching the additional sheep (hopefully) walk across the stage in an hour's time after a bit of tuneless singing and self-righteous preaching.

Then I can settle down to a nice uninterrupted game of 'Candy Crush' on my phone, or better still, a good texting session with BF.

Whilst amusing yourself in this way, it is very important to remember the following:

1) Put your phone on silent

2) Do not laugh out loud when BF sends you funny text, especially if it is at the sad moment when the donkey is dying in the play.

3) Do not let PM (who also becomes 'Pious and Godly' when in the church), see you amusing yourself.

4) You must remember to clap at the end.

5) You must remember to collect your child.

Although a little snack can also help to relieve the boredom, it is best if the snack is not in a loud, rustley packet, because most Good Parents do *not* eat snacks at the school play. The last thing you want in the middle of an absorbing game of Candy Crush is a Paddington Hard Stare from Pious and Godly Parents.

#6 Enduring School Sports Days

BTMs do not like sports days. In fact they live in dread of them. We are especially offended by the new political correctness surrounding sports days which dictate the following:

- Nobody is allowed to 'win'.

- It must be 'fair'.

- Egg and spoon races can't use eggs as they may break and a child might fall over and cut themselves on the eggshell, or be allergic to it and die.

- Parents are expected to participate in the adults' race.

Whatever.

Unfortunately, you cannot apply the same strategies that you use at the school play. It is far too obvious to get your phone out and play Candy Crush in the middle of the sports field as everyone will look at you and notice, plus it's a bit bright outside.

The pain of sports day seems to start with the multiple changes of days due to the British weather. This means that parents who have other commitments, i.e. all of us, have to endlessly rearrange work/ family/ lolling about, to fit in with watching their child lose, yet again.

Naturally, Perfect Mother's children are always the winners. They have the longest legs, eggs which stick to the spoon with glue like precision, and are generally popular, with the crowd urging them to win.

It is not 'sporting' to sit in the front row and stick your leg out, or casually misplace your large handbag in order to trip up the happy child running at the front belonging to the Competitive or Perfect Mother.

Some BTMs can see this as an opportunity to have a sneaky glass of wine in a thermos flask. The BTM's children are always lurking around at the back of the field normally wearing mismatched socks and in emergency-school-uniform-issue PE kit.

My favourite moment was when my youngest child, Charley was too hefty and lazy to properly join in with the sack race. Once all the other children had finished she was still shuffling along in her sack halfway down the track. She was rescued by two teachers, it needed two as she was, shall we say, 'challenging to lift' at that age. They took one side of the sack each and bounced her along the track, finishing with tumultuous applause.

Being the kind and caring mother that I am I videoed it for her so she could enjoy it in the future.

When it came to the part where it was time for the Mums' Race, I noticed all the Perfect Mothers becoming quickly reincarnated as Head Girls and sport swats, limbering up and doing stretches at the side of the field.

Naturally my children were keen to see me puff along behind the sylph like athletes. I think they believed I would win.

In order to avoid disappointing them, once the race started, I merely sauntered about waving at them, heading in the general direction of the finish line. After the race I was able to tell them that I had been so distracted waving to them I had not noticed the race had started.

Kudos to me. No hot sweaty face. Happy children.

#7 Laundry Avoidance

I think these tips work for any large family, but to be frank, I would have used this system if I had one child with three outfits. (If I am completely honest, I haven't ironed since being forced to iron hankies by my mother, when I was a resentful teenager).

- Do not iron under any circumstances.

- Always buy iron free clothing for the children

- Get reverse action tumble drier

- Don't have anything that will melt in the tumble drier as IRTs are famous for shoving everything from washing machine to tumble drier without checking.

Allocate one washing day per week per child. This has fantastic benefits.

- You know whose knickers are whose (less fighting)

- The Arguing Children stop chucking all the clothes in the washing basket when they can't be bothered to put them away. (If they do, they know they won't see those clothes again for a week).

- You know whose pockets the chewing gum/condom/illicit material came from. No question.

You also need to have a 'sock bin': You might buy 25 pairs of clean white socks one week and be left facing 16 unmatched socks in assorted colours with black, ground in dirt the next week. After years spent trying to re match them, asking pointless questions like;

- "Well where is the other one then?"

- "Why?"

- "Do you actually eat your socks?"

I learnt to wash all the socks and chuck them in the sock bin. The children then had the responsibility of matching them up themselves.

This led to some interesting events, including the famous 'one sock on- one sock off' debacle.

My children have not worn matching socks for some while, (they hadn't for some time before I introduced 'the sock bin') but who cares? Life's too short.

I know that the Perfect Mothers' children wear dazzling white, matching socks, probably with sweet lacy bits on the top, but really this is just showing off, unnecessary and petty.

#8 Guide to Christmas

Be unavailable at Christmas. Go abroad without your children if at all possible.

(Note to Therapeutic Parents currently in the thick of it: This WILL happen one day, but then you won't want to go as you won't want to miss the joy of experiencing Christmas with your securely attached grandchildren).

Christmas is to be endured not enjoyed. If you start off with this attitude, and make sure you have low expectations then anything more is a lovely surprise!

#9 Diminishing Christmas Present Drudgery

All parents are forced to 'celebrate' the commercial version of Christmas whether they want to or not. I prefer Ramadan. I mean THAT is a really great idea. I would love it if I didn't have to feed my Arguing Children for days on end, and then they had to go to the Mosque immediately after eating. Oh Bliss. Deep joy. Peace on Earth.

Unfortunately, I am compelled to 'do' Christmas. I am propelled into it by a plethora of adverts, homing in on unsuspecting AC and their resistant parents.

When my AC produce Argos catalogues with carefully circled items and pages left strategically open, I put it in the bin. Every BTM will find this a truly liberating experience. Not for the BTM the anguish of hunting down this year's must have toy. It is so much easier when you rule out:

- Anything the AC have asked for, on the grounds that they need to have 'a surprise'

- Anything with batteries, on the grounds that they will run out on Christmas Day afternoon and cause arguments. (Plus William used to eat them)

- Anything that can be used as a weapon

- Anything that needs to be 'assembled'

- Anything with dreadful packaging.

Most products then.

This may lead a Good and Patient Parent to believe that there is nothing left.

There is. It is called eBay.

By buying second hand gifts off eBay they arrive already assembled. The BTM can tell her children she is proud of them for doing their bit for recycling, and that they are to ignore the scratches on the Barbie bus.

We soon learnt to laboriously remove all packaging before wrapping the presents. This was an excellent idea until the toy did not work and had to be returned in 'original packaging'.

#10 ~~Not~~ Cooking Christmas Dinner

Under no circumstances should BTMs ever cook Christmas dinner. I *did* try.

There might have been a few futile attempts, very early on in parenting years. Those were the years when the rosy cheeked, dressing-gowned children, peeped bright-eyed around the door to see if Santa had been. In these early Christmas years, it was possible to play carols and look hopefully at the sky for the elusive globally-warmed snow.

Years later, when the Incredibly Rude Teenagers were sleeping in because Christmas was 'boring', I sat alone with a 7am sherry, toasting my bemused dogs. At this point I decided that we were 'going out' for Christmas Dinner next year.

The subsequent year at the restaurant, Patient Husband remarked that the dinner was not 'as good' as my Christmas Dinner. The IRTs were too busy troughing the food and giving each other sly kicks under the table, to even notice who cooked it.

At this point any BTM doesn't give a toss anymore. She is just so thrilled to know she can return home shortly, feeling slightly drunk, and still be able to see her kitchen work tops.

From here on in, most Christmases go ok. The presents have been opened and for once this just about meets your children's overwhelming emotional needs. Just Christmas. Everyday.

Plus, you can now legitimately drink wine in the day time.

#11 Fun Family Days Out

As a Therapeutic Parent I tried really hard to avoid fun family days out. This is because I learned fast that there is no such thing. (See later chapter on 'Holidays').

Well to be fair there might be one or two that happen very occasionally and these will be videoed and photographed as evidence of having had fun once, together as a family.

Although the BTM spends quite a lot of her time trying to organise things which will distract the children from arguing, it often appears that the fun family days out mainly consist of;

- Lengthy car ride with Arguing Children

- Lengthy queueing with moaning children

- Lengthy packed lunches with bossy children.

- Outdoor lunches, on tiny patches of grass, avoiding wasps and flies as AC run round screaming hysterically.

It quickly becomes clear why the best person to organise and manage the Fun Family Day Out is the Ignorant Non Parent. Sometimes, in these particular circumstances, more kindly referred to as the *Unsuspecting* Non Parent.

This is usually a maiden aunt, or best friend, hoping to have children with her boyfriend and convince him that they will have a great time as parents. Remember 'The Parenthood Lie'?

Fun Days Out with practicing-to-be-parents are a good way to avoid Fun *Family* Days Out altogether. The day is short, the children momentarily distracted from arguing and it may *appear* to be quite jolly on the surface. The BTM can wave her children happily off knowing that she now has time for a nice cup of tea and a few hours of silence.

#12 Eating Out ~~to Avoid Cooking~~

When my children were small, eating out consisted of finding restaurants where there were soft play areas. You know the ones? They have a sweaty little hole full of plastic balls that you deposit your children into. Then you make a vain attempt to have a meal or a cup of coffee or anything that will keep you going till bedtime.

There is no point whatsoever, going to restaurants where normal people eat. This is a waste of your time and furthermore it is cruel to the people who have tried to get away from their children only to be confronted with your badly behaved Arguing Children. Let's face it we have already established in Part One that we don't like it so let's not do it to everybody else. There is a reason for the existence of McDonald's.

I used to be able to guarantee that when I was out with my children in some kind of pseudo upmarket melange of McDonald's & Harvester horror, the waiters would become the least observant at times of maximum need. I.e. if I went in and the children were very hungry (like, every time), I knew that the waiters would suddenly be exceptionally busy, polishing glasses and removing specks of dust from adjacent tables.

Luckily Rosie Rudey learned really quickly from me the best way to deal with eye-contact-avoiding-waiters. She would simply see my huffing and sighing face and immediately walk up to the bar and say loudly, "I think everyone has forgotten table number 12."

The children and I soon found that another good strategy to make sure that waiters would serve us quickly was to do 'pretend' naughty behaviour. If there was an unacceptable gap between dinner and pudding, on my cue, the children would start to misbehave. They would swing on chairs, or give pokes to each other and increase the general noise level. This guaranteed swift intervention by the waiters who were keen to see the back of us.

Amazingly, sometimes I did not even *need* to ask my children to behave badly as they obliged without being asked at all.

After three years, (during a trip to Florida), I found the best way of eating out was- buffet all the way! This was an amazing breakthrough. I could arrive at the restaurant and be on my way home again within 45 minutes. Naturally I had to put very strict boundaries around the acceptable height to pile food on one's plate, but other than that it was invariably a successful family outing.

Perfect for BTMs with Arguing Children in fact.

#13 ~~Not~~ Sewing

At school I spent two years pretending to sew one dress. I realised that if I sat quietly in the corner miming a sewing action, the teacher basically left me alone. At the end of two years the dress I was supposedly making was still only tacked together. It would no longer have fitted me. This was a great disappointment to my own patchwork-and-quilting-seamstress-extraordinaire mother.

Needless to say I am not a sewing kind of mother. I think Perfect Mothers and Baking-Mothers-With-Clipboard are the kind of mothers who do sewing. Not BTMs, and definitely not very busy Therapeutic Parents.

When my children were growing up, I found the best way to avoid sewing was to simply replace the clothes, although this did get quite expensive. I was thrilled when they brought out Teflon trousers but sadly discovered they weren't actually made from frying pans, which is what I had hoped. William Wobbly, therefore, was able to continue tearing and chewing holes the size of tennis balls into the majority of his clothing on most days. (See Part 3 Chapter 16 for Vagrant Dressing)

#14 Reducing Hospital Drudgery

Earlier on in this section I explained how being in hospital for oneself can actually feel like a bit of a spa break so I am not classing that as drudgery. In fact, one of the most restful weeks I ever had when the children were growing up, was the week I spent in hospital following a mild stroke.

It's a different story if you have to spend time in hospital with a child. Now, obviously if the child is genuinely very ill and it's a worrying time the last thing on your mind, (even if you *are* a BTM), is how boring it all is.

Probably.

Most of the time however, I found I was in hospital waiting for a child to have something extracted from their ear or nose, or to have two stitches for a fingertip cut. This is dullness and drudgery beyond endurance. Not only are you faced with the child seeking maximum input from you as trapped parent, for a not very serious illness - but there is literally nothing to do!

On top of that you know there are about 6 million jobs waiting to be done at home including drinking a large bottle of wine with your name on it.

The best way to minimise drudgery in the hospital is to avoid going there at all costs. You will find that your local GP is usually pretty handy at sending you to a local unit who will do little stitches and minor procedures. Ask yourself the question, 'Do we really need to go to the hospital?'

OK once my daughter DID actually have a broken shoulder and she was walking round a bit lopsided, but other than that I couldn't be expected to know. I might be a therapeutic BTM but I am not psychic.

The next possibility is to send someone in your place. Again, the Ignorant Non Parent, or Unsuspecting Non Parent is usually pretty good at going to the hospital for you - especially if you make it sound a bit dramatic and important.

If there is no way out and you really *do* have to go to the hospital, decide that you will be there for six hours. Take some headphones for you and the child, and always have some downloaded episodes of some vacuous nonsense on an iPad that you can quickly plug the child into. This at least stops nonsense chatter for short periods of time *and* constant references to the minor ailment, which obviously has practically 'killed' them.

My other top tip as a BTM is to ensure that you have a power pack in your bag for your phone. This means at the very least you can disappear off to the toilet for very long periods of time, lock yourself in and play Candy Crush.

#15 Avoiding Homework

I love this one. This is one of my favourites! When I talk about this at training, peoples' mouths drop open in horror and surprise. This is quickly followed by gasps of pleasure and delight. (Teachers, miss this section out).

Breaking news: You do not *have* to do your child's homework! You do not have to sit down next to them for two hours out of your precious day to try to achieve an arduous 20 minutes of deep-pen-scouring 'work'. You don't have to keep trying to make it look like they are more intelligent than they are, to get them put in a higher grade.

Step away. Stop. Do not do it.

When I realised that my children could not manage the transition of me changing from 'mummy' to 'teacher' and all the associated horrible behaviours that went with it. I simply stopped doing homework all together.

My children did not die and I did not go to prison.

Yes, alright, the school *were* quite cross with me and summonsed me in. When I went in to see the Headmaster about my total lack of conformity, he asked me why my children were not doing their homework. I replied that I had asked them to do their homework and I had created space and time for them to do it however, unfortunately the children were too busy trying to make secure attachments or punching each other and at the end of a long, hard school day they were unable to focus on yet more school work. The Headmaster retorted that I should support the school and enforce their boundaries at home. I said,

"That is a brilliant idea! Can you please come round to my house at the weekend, tell the children to tidy their bedrooms and supervise them please? That will save me a load of work!"

The Headmaster expressed some consternation.

We came to a 'mutual understanding' - I would not be a teacher and he would not be a Therapeutic Parent.

As I suspected, my children all caught up later on, once their head were less busy and the arguing, punching and noise had diminished somewhat.

#16 ~~Not~~ Mending Things

All BTMs know that even when our children are not annoying us, there are plenty of other things to take their place. This is usually inanimate objects. This can be computers, iPads, printers, televisions, lawnmowers, toasters, cars etc.

It can be exhilarating and liberating to shout and scream at the inanimate object. This at least releases cortisol and enables us to get a grip slightly. Although it is also satisfying to smash objects up when they refuse to cooperate, it may be expensive and rarely solves the problem.

Amazingly, I have found that therapeutic parenting techniques appear to work on inanimate objects! I have often found myself doing 'empathic ignoring' on the computer. So- as it seizes up, goes into 'blank screen' or simply refuses to respond, I turn away, have a cup of tea, watch the screen slyly with my slidey eyes, and say out loud something like,

"I can see you are finding this difficult, but the sooner we start, the sooner you can rest."

An observer would think I had lost the plot, (I probably have), but it makes me feel better and invariably the computer starts to work. If you like, you can scream at it a bit as well first and then practice your therapeutic parenting on it. I have often found that I am in a mental state of 'teaching something a lesson' and suddenly realise it is an object which cannot possibly ever learn the lesson.

I don't care, it makes me feel better anyway.

#17 ~~Not~~ Going to the Gym

As if we don't have enough to do some of us are strange enough to create extra tasks and jobs. One such task the BTM sets herself all too often, is that of 'Going to the Gym'.

This is a *very* silly idea. This is something PMs do in their skin-tight leggings and matching tops. The skin tight leggings annoyingly accentuate their perfect little buttocks, displayed almost obscenely as they sashay away.....

As a rule, the best idea is to *pretend* to go to the gym and leave the house at a set time every day to go and sit on the comfy sofa somewhere, eating cake and drinking coffee.

I know many BTMs like me, also suffer from carrying excess weight due to our cortisol/stress overload which needs to be fuelled by sugar in the form of chocolate, cakes and other yummy things. Happy news though! Once the children have grown up and left home, the excess baggage seems to just melt away.

Unfortunately, when the BTM feels obliged to go to the gym it is normally at a time when all the children are at school or in bed, thereby wasting a precious hour which could be used on loving oneself and eating more chocolate.

I found the most effective way of using gym membership was to join the local gym and pay by direct debit. This meant that when my bank statement arrived there was an extra direct debit printed on my statement. Therefore, it was slightly heavier to carry, and consequently I was getting a workout, simply by paying the direct debit to the gym, and carrying the bank statement from the front door to the bin.

This was sufficient justification to enable me to go and have coffee and cake in Sainsbury's guilt free, instead of actually *going* to the gym. Patient Husband never appeared to notice that I failed to lose any weight.

Either that or he valued his life.

PART THREE:

MANAGING THE ARGUING CHILDREN

When Lazy Husband and I were assessed as adopters, I remember sitting opposite the Social Worker and smiling indulgently at her while she explained to me that in fact any children who we adopted were likely to be 'damaged' or 'needy' in some way. I felt quite smug really. After all, I was a qualified 'children and families' social worker. I understood the background of children who are adopted. I had carried out assessments for Foster Carers, I had fostered. I had worked in therapeutic children's homes, (many of them caring for children from adoption breakdowns). I had had step children. I thought I knew it all. The assessing social worker talked about 'Challenging Behaviour'. I didn't actually realise what that meant. You might have thought I would. My idea of 'challenging behaviour' roughly translated into 'parents who can't manage their children'. Super Nanny had nothing on me. People used to take me on holiday with them because I was the only person who could get their children to behave.

So when the social worker went on (and on) about how difficult we might find some of the behaviours, I sat there mentally tapping my fingers and wondering if I could politely take yet another custard cream off the plate without appearing to have an eating disorder.

Of course I had heard about the famous 'Honeymoon Period', but I did not know this was a lie. It's actually more of a 'Buy your tickets, sit in front row, then be reluctant to leave when real show starts' kind of thing.

#1 Fantasy vs Reality

When I thought about becoming a mother I imagined Enid Blyton type picnics with children frolicking around me in the sunshine, wearing spotless white dresses and matching socks. We would be drinking ginger beer, consuming cheese sandwiches, apples and carrots politely, (with mouths closed). The children would never complain about what they had to eat and would be playing nicely together.

Instead of spiffing adventures and obedient children playing hide and seek in un-chewed clothes, I found myself thrust into a world with a surround sound audio of Arguing Children playing on a loop. If you are making an Enid Blyton picnic that means you have to go to Tesco's to buy all the ingredients, *with* the Arguing Children.

This is not a nice start to the picnic. It can only go one way from here.

#2 Feeding the Arguing Children

PMs cook healthy meals for their children, who naturally never argue. These meals are mostly organic and often vegetarian. The GM does not mind accommodating her children's varying tastes by cooking several different meals simultaneously according to;

- Their tastes,

- The time they can be expected in.

The BTM on the other hand cannot always be relied upon to provide a meal of any description at the given time. This is because she is:

- Selfishly at work

- Selfishly at the supermarket still waiting in the checkout queue

- Selfishly (and grudgingly) dealing with the latest ill child at the hospital

- Selfishly attending yet another meeting with the school who 'have concerns'.

If the parent is trying to do therapeutic parenting, it only makes them more bad-tempered as they know how important routine is. The BTM takes the view that the AC can 'bloody well eat what I give them'. She also believes that AC should experiment with new tastes, even if this does mean mixing tinned macaroni cheese with beetroot.

The BTM has even been known to put chili sauce or pickled onions in her AC's food in order to 'make them be a bit more adventurous'. This usually happens around the time when a fussy child announces that they 'only want to eat beige food', or that food items 'must not touch.'

When Sophie Spikey announced this new rule to me I quickly got the blender out and mixed it all together.

"There you go," I said, "separate that!"

She did not mention food 'touching' again.

BTMs usually encourage food independence at the earliest opportunity. This is great because obviously it is dressed up as 'helping them to become more independent, empower them, give them more choice' etc. In actual fact every BTM will know that really it equates to, 'I cannot face one more day of making sandwiches which will only become penicillin by Tuesday.'

#3 Encouraging the AC to ~~Go Away~~ Play Out

I was so relieved when new research suggested that we should be making our children play out and take more risks, in order that they 'learned'. As a BTM I had been saying this myself for years but the Mummy Mafia had always looked at me askance, silently condemning me for 'not caring' about my children.

Now I knew that not only could I tell my children to go out to play with impunity, but I could also make comments about how sad it was that Natasha and Casper had failed to 'learn' through playing out, and remark on their paleness.

We moved to the countryside in order to achieve 'playing out'. We were surrounded by fields, streams and 'climby' trees. When I ejected the Arguing Children from the house, surgically removing their tech and phones, they spent months with their sullen, reproachful faces flattened against the window. They should have known I would never surrender.

Prising them off the back door and into the world of 'playing out adventures' was not an easy journey. I found myself prancing about in meadows like an hysterical Julie Andrews, holding frenzied picnics, demonstrating how to climb the big trees, looking down at their baffled faces, while I screeched about the fun I was having up the tree.

Long lost childhood adventures were revisited for the children's amusement. Stickleback fishing in the stream, making dens, throwing together rope swings.

I steered clear of bonfires.

At the end of it all I was exhausted. The children continued munching the bribe picnic silently, eyeing me warily.

Trudging home I felt like a BT-Failure-Mother. The Arguing Children continued bickering unperturbed, looking forwards to being reunited with their tech and duvets.

The next day, however, I had my revenge. The Wi-Fi was switched off and I announced breezily that it was 'Playing Out time' until midday. Against a backdrop of indignant shrieks and threats to contact ChildLine, I busied myself with urgent pseudo tidying, which included unplugging all electrical devices for 'cleaning'.

I reminded the AC that they now knew where the climby trees were, how to catch sticklebacks and the best place for making rope swings. I waved cheerfully as they trudged out as one, in a large sulky lump.

Two hours later at exactly midday, they walked the 20 metres from our front wall (where they had all been sitting since being expelled from the house), to the door, and morosely re-entered the kitchen exclaiming how exhausted they were.

I didn't care. I had had 2 hours of peace. The arguing had been very faint indeed with the doors and windows shut.

Well it *is* a fact that respite frees the brain.

#4 Leaving the Arguing Children

The first time, I decided I would leave the house for 20 minutes in order to encourage the AC to remove their faces from the side of the house, I struck a deal before I left, along the lines of; "You play out for one hour and I'll take you to the fete this afternoon."

When I returned it was clear that most of the children had failed in their attempts to 'play out'. I realised this because:

- One was lying supine on the doorstep,

- Three were lying face down on the trampoline arguing,

- One had allegedly 'just got back.'

- Two children had been playing a 'strangling' game

- William had been to the shops crossing the forbidden main road.

As well as these small incidents, Katie had pretended to walk the dogs returning home immediately after our exit in order to attempt a kind of political coo, establishing herself as 'Mother Superior' and generally winding everyone up. Sophie had appeared to play nicely but neglected to mention the injured child left on the trampoline, crying and alone. Rosie Rudey, cast in the role of 'spy', (in an attempt to try to stop her being the fat controller), had actually done some revision and was thrilled to inform us that 'no one had gone out to play' and indeed, 'everyone had in fact been very naughty'.

I informed the transgressors that unfortunately their presence would no longer be required at the fete, as they had 'playing out' to do. This resulted in much screaming and abuse as Incredibly Rude Teenager 1 (Katie) stormed out of the house accusing me of 'changing the rules.'

IRT 2 (William) then also left 'to walk the dog', and subsequently failed to return. Surprisingly, the dog appeared to be at home. I was clearly supposed to be very worried and call the police to mount a search party. Instead I chose to take advantage of the sudden lull in screaming accusations by reading the newspaper and eating chocolate.

Only a *true* BTM can achieve this level of nonchalance when one (or hopefully more), of their children absconds.

#5 Accepting a New 'Normal'

Post placement, it is easier if would-be Therapeutic Parents simply accept that their lives are now often fraught with danger and stress, and prepare to welcome in the BTM dark side.

Sometimes, emergency self- extraction is called for in times of crisis. Normally this is at the point where drama and disaster are followed in quick succession by tragedy and catastrophe..... So most days then if you are an aspiring Therapeutic Parent....

One afternoon Rosie Rudey came home making loud banging and sighing noises. She unwrapped the cake she had made at school and placed it proudly on the kitchen table. I (finally) made the correct noises about it being 'lovely' and reassured her that even soggy, damp cakes (dropped on way home) often taste quite nice.

This is the absolute maximum amount of parental encouragement any BTM can possibly muster at such a fraught hour in the day.

I returned home from picking up the remaining AC to find that one of the dogs had eaten over half of Rosie's cake. The dog was still fiercely protecting the remaining half from the other six circling dogs, pretending starvation, having been fed 1 hour ago. Rosie was furious.

The greediest child (Charley Chatty), was devastated about the prospective loss of cake, and started negotiating hard about 'cutting bits off' in order to remove the dog slobber.

Rosie began removing bits of cake with dog drool on. She then started to show me her English course work in an effort to ensure that I did not engage in any meaningful way with the other children.

Hand-grenade child Sophie, helpfully pointed out that:

- Charley had stolen some slobbered on cake and was eating it under the table,

- William had just licked the remaining cake to claim ownership,

- The cake tasted disgusting

- Katie appeared to be missing

I knew Katie was not missing because I could hear an incoherent stream of nonsense chatter floating up from the garden.

I pasted a loving and interested expression on my face, and sipped my tea slowly, nodded periodically and then feigned sleep.

Naturally this prompted an immediate escalation in noise levels from AC, so a swift exit to a locked bathroom was called for.

A loud radio assists at these times. As does a large glass of wine.

5 Avoiding Nonsense-Chatter Madness

Most adopters and foster parents have to put up with nonsense chatter to a degree never experienced by birth parents. You know the normal stage children go through when they are two or three and they say all kinds of nonsense things? Well times that by about 2 million, let it go on for about 10 years and that's what you are facing as a Therapeutic Parent, with a child participating in the Nonsense Chatter Olympic games.

Some of the most memorable topics my children spoke about during 'nonsense chatter triathlons' were:

- Is that a mountain? -when going up a chairlift in a ski resort

- Is that a plane? -when landing at an airport.

- Are we in the swimming pool? - When standing waist deep in the swimming pool.

You get the picture?

Unfortunately, it was not just the odd question it was an endless, streaming bombardment of total nonsense assaulting my ears and brain. It took me a while to realise that I did not *have to* answer this stupid nonsense.

As I BTM it was surprisingly easy to disengage and ignore. I fantasised about getting some duct tape and using it to good effect, but I thought that I might get in trouble from social services if I did that. Instead I made up happy little songs in my head which quickly transmogrified into headphones welded to my ears. I would tell my children I was learning a new song and swiftly put my headphones on playing loud, screamy opera music.

As I became more skilled in therapeutic parenting I learnt a couple of good tactics. I would tell the nonsense chatterer that my ears were full up, but that I would have capacity to listen to her at exactly 4pm. When 4pm came I would sit down all agog, pen poised ready to take notes on the very exciting nonsense chatter. Naturally the child was completely silent. There would be the occasional lack lustre attempt at engaging me with, "Ummm…. Errr…" look to ceiling, "At school today, ummm, errrr….." etc.

Five minutes later when the nonsense chatter started again I would say, "Oh dear! I am sorry you have used up the time today. I have no more space left for nonsense words only important ones."

Naive others, Patronising Professionals and Ignorant Non Parents, would no doubt have looked on in horror and accused me of child abuse, but let's be honest, they don't have to live with it.

#6 Paying Back the Incredibly Rude Teenager

When your slightly overweight teenager decides to try wearing 'hot-pants' for the first time, it's *not* ok to say they look more like 'Cold- Porky–Pants.' There are more subtle ways to pay them back.

I have no clue what God was thinking about when he put Bad-Tempered Mothers and Incredibly Rude Teenagers in the same house. It is some kind of sick joke, especially if the IRT is a girl, and her PMT coincides with her BTM's.

As a self-confessed Incredibly BTM I have found that the best strategy for dealing with an IRT is to sing or scream loudly. This drowns out the nasty comments and entreaties to 'get a life you sad bitch' quite nicely I find.

The GM will sit her IRT down and talk to her about how she feels when IRT is so unkind to her. If I had used this strategy with my children I might as well have walked about with a target on my back saying, 'shoot me here.'

The BTM's approach is far more satisfying and less time consuming. She doesn't have to engage with the IRT on any level during the rudeness phase. It is just unfortunate that the rudeness is there all the time, apart from sleeping periods.

IRT (William) was in a very bad mood because I had had the audacity to ask him to do three things in a row:

1) Tidy his room

2) Put his plate in the dishwasher

3) Go and have a shower.

This provoked a lot of grumbling and threatening. Eventually he went into the bathroom muttering, (as loud as he dared) 'Dog breath', which I pretended not to hear in the interests of world peace.

There was much banging and some breaking noises coming from the shower. I listened attentively, creeping off periodically to make loud singing noises elsewhere. (Subliminal message, 'I am happy, I can't hear you'). When William emerged from the shower, PH discovered that he had turned all the dials to 'cold' in order that the next person using the shower experienced a nasty shock. PH turned the dials to 'warm', then had his shower. Afterwards, he was careful to return the dials to 'cold' in order not to upset William.

PH knows that every BTM needs their IRT to have consequences for their actions.

The next day, William went to have his shower. Cue hysterical shrieking. When he came out he informed us that the shower had been 'freezing' and he had had to get out of the shower to switch it off by the pull cord in order to adjust it. We wondered out loud together as to the cause of this event, exploring several possibilities and struggling not to let the smug smile slide onto our faces.

#7 ~~Enjoying~~ Managing Absconding

I have explained how the BTM quite enjoys it when her Arguing Children abscond because it gives her time for quiet reflection and a cup of tea.

It does depend on the age and stage of the child, so for example, I was quite relaxed when my teenagers absconded to go and play on other peoples' PlayStations and eat their biscuits, but I was less relaxed when my 12-year-old ran away to the local drunkard's house.

It is possible to use your other children as spies when you have one child who absconds. If you actually *do* want them to come back quickly, then you simply bribe the other children to find them. Their contacts are much better than yours and they are more adept at applying social media etc.

When Charley was an IRT- in-training, she left the house in a rage because I had selfishly asked her to tidy her bedroom. By 'tidy' I meant remove anything actually mouldy or infested.

When I made the simple mistake of then saying she was grounded, understandably she just walked out. I quickly learnt not to do this in the future. (Far better to say, "Get out right now!" and then they will plant themselves firmly in the house).

Anyway, two of my sneaky-spy children, William and Sophie located her very efficiently within 30 minutes and were duly rewarded with extra TV time.

I went round to the house knocked at the door and walked straight in saying, "Is my daughter here?"

The drunk woman who answered the door couldn't really focus or stand upright so I went straight up the stairs. I found Charley cuddled up in bed ready for a good night's sleep, along with her 12-year-old 'new best friend' (of 45 minutes), in the other single bed.

In this situation the BTM has only one line of action. We have to shout very loudly. "GET OUT RIGHT NOW!!"

(Note to adopters and foster parents this is *not* therapeutic parenting, this is called 'out of control screaming shoutyness').

It was quite effective though and Charley shot out of the bed as if propelled by a rocket. I marched her out of the house in her pyjamas pausing only to tell the parent, "If you ever so much as look at my daughter again, I will have you locked up."

I didn't quite know how I would achieve this because by now I was fairly certain that according to Patronising Professionals, anything that went slightly awry was definitely my fault.

This meant that future absconding episodes by Charley did not involve third parties. She reverted back to the usual 'lurking round the garden' variety.

Much nicer for everyone.

#9 Packed Lunches

When my children were small it was very easy to do lovely little healthy packed lunches. Understandably the school nutrition mafia would inspect their lunchboxes regularly to ensure that I did not ever include anything that should be remotely sugary or tasty to eat.

Once they became Incredibly Rude Teenagers, the whole issue of packed lunches became a nightmare which made my bad-temperedness increase at the very thought of preparing them. A mere few hours would pass before the healthy packed lunch would be discarded disdainfully, only to become festering green penicillin at the bottom of the schoolbag, or under the bed.

I got round this by allocating each child a small budget with which to buy their own ingredients for their packed lunch. This meant there was less likelihood of rotting fruit being found, although we probably did end up with shares in the sausage roll factory.

My top packed lunch strategies now are basically:

1) Don't do packed lunches unless you absolutely have to.
2) See above

I understand that you do absolutely *have* to, when your child spends all their pocket money or dinner money in the shop on the way to school, and then tells everyone they are hungry (with a sad 'ChildLine' face). But if you do *have* to do packed lunches for teens, don't bother putting in anything;

- That can go off.
- Is easily hidden.
- That is deemed 'healthy'.

The fact that your child will invariably nip off down the chip shop anyway, telling all their friends they have no dinner and pleading starvation, is a given.

#10 Living in Harmony with Death Risk Bedrooms

I know that Perfect Mothers have perfect children with perfect bedrooms I have even visited some of my friends' houses and exclaimed in surprise when going into the children's bedrooms and finding that they don't smell and you can still see the floor.

This is not the case in my house or any other BTM's house that I have seen.

Even after my children had all left for school, every time I had to pass the bedroom doors I would be assaulted by the smells of rotting food, unwashed socks, urine and other unmentionables which I don't even want to think about any more.

Basically you have two choices you can either;

- Tidy your children's bedroom yourself every single day, going through everything to ensure that there are no stashes of food, drink, drugs, cigarettes and alcohol.

- You can simply shut the door and never look at it again.

Naturally, being a control freak, initially I used option one, but quickly realised that consuming cups of tea and cake were a preferable way to spend my time, and closing the door took only four seconds.

With sneakily timed pocket money and outings I was able to ensure the children did *actually* tidy their bedrooms to a non-hazardous level at key moments.

#11 Mad Lying

Right up there with any form of stealing comes the lying, or 'mad lying' as I like to call it.

This is another one of those behaviours where parents of securely attached birth children really should just BE QUIET.

'Mad' lying is not the same as standard lying. Therapeutic Parents are faced with mad lying on a daily basis, usually many times per day. Just so that everyone is clear, here are some examples of mad lies told to me by my children:

- 'I did NOT put any sugar in my tea' -after video evidence played back to child showing 16 spoonful's of sugar being put into tea less than 5 minutes ago. Child still holding cup of syrupy tea.

- 'I did not even TOUCH the biscuits' - while still holding the empty packet, chocolate and crumbs round mouth.

- 'My mother has had a heart attack and is in hospital' (homework avoidance tactic). When the teacher and I (blatantly healthy mother), confronted the perpetrator she insisted that I had 'forgotten' being in hospital.

Over the years I have seen mad lying become the cause of many parents' bad-temperedness. It is especially frustrating because the children we care for *have* to argue and lie like their lives depend on it.

In the early days, as an unskilled traditional Super-Nanny type, I would insist the child would 'sit there till they admitted the truth'. This got very boring very quickly and I never resolved anything, so I quickly invented new ways.

My vocabulary flourished with lovely little trite sayings, enabling me to acknowledge the lie, disengage and walk away. Phrases like:

- I expect you are right

- That is a shame for you because now…

- Fancy that!

This just about kept me on an even keel and the children did not see the steam coming out of my ears as I smiled happily and turned away.

My favourite mad lie won my admiration for tenacity, duration (2 days), and creativity.

Katie, age 12 came home from school wearing bright pink stilettos. Now I was fairly confident that the school had not changed its uniform policy to incorporate this so naturally I enquired where they had come from. Katie claimed that her 'friend' (she did not have any) had 'lent them to her.'

I am sure you know that Therapeutic Parents are also ace detectives. Katie was also aware of this but had clearly decided to take a risk. Turning the shoes over, I saw on the bottom a price tag, £20, and the store sticker 'New Look'.

"Hmm that's interesting," I said "Rosie had a voucher for 'New Look' for £20 but it went missing yesterday. What a coincidence!"

The blotches immediately appearing on Katie's face were all the confirmation I needed. This was instantly followed by screeches and screams protesting her innocence. Sighing inwardly, (there was a glass of wine with my name on it in the fridge), I used some of my standard phrases, 'Fancy that! ….. Anyway I have decided that you took the voucher so we will need to think of a way for you to reimburse Rosie.' In the meantime, I stated that I would be looking after the pink stilettos.

This was swiftly followed by claims that the 'friend' who had given her the shoes would be 'furious' and would 'probably punch her'. The worn-out-BTM part of me allowed myself to indulge in that little fantasy for a short, unhealthy moment.

The following day, wine consumed and feeling stronger, I raised the issue of compensation for Rosie again, along with my expectations, and asked Katie if she had had any ideas yet. I knew this would be the catalyst for apoplectic, indignant screaming, but I was mentally prepared. Amazingly, Katie said,

"Ok I am going to tell you the truth." (I had to sit down quickly).

Katie said, "I DID take the voucher but only because I was being bullied at school."

For a wonderful second I thought there might be some truth in this and Katie was *actually* 'doing a deep and meaningful' but luckily I quickly got a grip before hope took hold.

"Well," I said, "I need to come to the school and help you sort this out. Who is bullying you?"

Katie – "I don't know his name."

Me- "Ok well what has he said? How has he bullied you?"

Katie – "He said I had to take Rosie's voucher."

Me -…. "And buy a pair of pink stilettos…?"

Katie – "Yes."

Me – "For *you* to wear?"

Katie – "Yes, he has been bullying me for months."

Me – "Well this sounds very serious. I am going to come to the school and speak to this boy."

Katie (panicking) – "But I don't know his name!"

Me – "That's ok. I will just stand at the entrance with you watching everyone come in and out and you can just point him out. Then I will go and ask him what on earth he was thinking of, bullying my daughter into buying herself a pair of pink stilettos!"

Katie (becoming more blotchy)- "No… but I can't remember what he looks like!"

Me – "So to summarise. You have been bullied for months by a boy you don't recognise and don't know the name of. He somehow knew your sister had a £20 voucher and forced you to steal it. He then forced you to use the voucher on something that he could never possibly want or use. Have I got this right?"

Silence, closely followed by shriek of, "You NEVER believe me!!"

At this point I did manage to give Katie a spade to dig herself out of her lie-hole, as I needed to urgently return to being the referee, (in order to reduce the screaming and punching noises coming from downstairs).

Me – "I think you have got a bit mixed up. The main thing we need to do is put it right with Rosie so I will take half your pocket money until it's paid back."

As I managed to extract a mute nod of agreement, I achieved a brief one way rigid-hug and exited quickly before a new lie could appear.

I returned to the fray, pausing only briefly to perform a slidey slump, silently against the wall on the way down the stairs.

Sometimes my children would tell lies which had a kernel of truth within them. One day, Charley came home from school and told me that she had in fact 'saved her friends life'. *(See Charley Chatty and the Wiggly Worry Worm, Sarah Naish and Rosie Jefferies, Jessica Kingsley Publishing).* Her friend was two years younger than her. She told me that they had been playing in the woods and a man had to come in and grabbed her little friend.

Initially I felt some consternation, but then luckily remembered that I was dealing with somebody who lived in a fantasy world for the majority of the day. I asked Charley how she had managed to save her friend's life. She told me that she had 'kicked the man in the head.'

At the time, Charley was 7, very short and..... well, dumpy. I wondered aloud how such a small person had managed to kick a man in the head. I asked her if she could act it out with me.

I must admit to suppressing some mirth while I acted out the part of the man, having to lower myself first to my knees and then bending down even further in order to facilitate Charley 'kicking me in the head.'

As she kicked higher and higher, blatantly missing the target spot of 'head' by some inches, the last vigorous kick took her clean off her feet and into a crumpled heap on the floor.

We mutually agreed that the incident had probably not happened and Charley had somehow been confused.

12 ~~Sugar Stealing~~ Food Management

Charley went to school very early on school dinner-money day. On return I asked her what she had had for lunch and her 'lying face' said, "Cheese and tomato pasta'". I asked why I had seen her in Tesco express and she lied that various people, (including Sophie), 'forced' her to go and buy chocolate hobnobs. After emptying the school bag and finding a packet of empty jelly babies and a chocolate ripple, she finally produced half packet of biscuits in a flourish of honesty.

The next day Charley stole a pot of jam. Patient Husband saw it when he woke her up, lying next to her in bed like some kind of 'Art Moderne' teddy. When he challenged her about it she said, "Its ok mummy knows I am stealing food." As I had also found three yoghurt pots in her school bag 2 days prior, in Charley-Land, my prior knowledge therefore exonerated her from any further responsibility.

One of the things that used to make me the most bad-tempered was when I had saved a special treat for myself and I would wait for an opportune moment to go and have said treat only to find they had been:

- stolen

- spoiled

- licked

- snotted on

- poked with a finger, leaving bogey fingerprint dent

- all of the above

This meant that I had to get very good at hiding any little treats that I wanted to keep for myself.

It didn't matter that the child might have actually *given* me the chocolates themselves, (aided and abetted by Patient Husband). If they were left unattended I could guarantee that all the lovely chocolates would (mysteriously) disappear, leaving only the Snickers and Bounty rejects in the tin.

The safe in my bedroom did not just contain cash, it contained packets of special biscuits, little packets of chocolate, and even the occasional doughnut.

Occasionally I forgot about the doughnut. That did not have a good ending. Patient Husband did not like having to scrape the green penicillin doughnut off his cash.

By the time all the children were teenagers I had to take self-preserving action. The padlocks came out for the fridge and one cupboard. In this way I could also ensure there were packed lunches for the week and the odd treat that had been earned.

Granted this strategy did not last very long because I found better ones, but the BTM part of me found myself gazing with love and satisfaction at the shiny new padlock on the sweet cupboard.

On one occasion Charley surpassed herself. She had bought some chocolates for her friend for Christmas. When I discovered this I said to her,

"There is no way those chocolates will last from now until Christmas Day! Do you want me to look after them for you?"

Obviously I knew I would probably eat them myself but at least I would quickly be able to replace them before she noticed. Charley declined, doubtless feeling her chocolates were safer left with her than with me.

She may have had a point.

When it came to the day where presents were wrapped and about to be sent out, I picked up the present for her friend. I knew it should weigh the equivalent of a box of chocolates. Instead it weighed about the same as an *empty* box of chocolates.

I carefully removed the wrapping paper and opened the box. Inside, all of the chocolates had been eaten apart from the hazelnut whirls. One had clearly been sampled. I have no idea if Charley had actually intended to deliver the present to the child at school. No doubt the hazelnut whirls would also have met a non-Christmassy end….. (Apart from a little fat person saying 'Ho, ho ho!')

In order to help Charley learn about consequences (and to supply myself with a good laugh), I removed the present from the pile, told her I had seen the child's mother and had hand-delivered it myself.

Cue gasp of horror and learning experience.

My favourite stories always seem to combine stealing food with a bit of mad lying. Once I had become a bit more skilled in therapeutic parenting, and stopped having exploding rages, I could have a bit of fun with this.

One day I returned home two minutes after Charley arrived back from school. I was with Sophie in the car and as we pulled into the drive, hand-grenade-child-Sophie said,

"Ooh I wonder how much food Charley has managed to eat in the last two minutes?!"

We entered the house to the smell of newly toasted toast. I went to the toaster placed my hand on it and asked,

"Oh did you decide to have some toast?'"

Charley immediately started screaming and shouting, 'It's not fair! Why are you picking on me? I wasn't the only one in the house!" etc.

I pointed out to her that in fact she *was* the only one in the house as I had just returned with Sophie. I also said I did not mind if she had some food and was just wondering if she had had anything. Charley turned and stomped up the stairs, making sure that they shook with each ascending step.

I went to put something in the bin and as I opened it I saw three slices of steaming, warm toast sitting on the top. I took them out and placed them on the breakfast bar behind me. When Charley came back down the stairs, I said,

"If you are hungry when you come in from school its fine if you have some fruit or a piece of toast. I don't want you to have more than one piece before dinner though."

Charley returned to screaming accusations- 'always picking on her, she wasn't even there, she had not put any toast in the toaster, she was entirely innocent of all toast related events' etc. I produced the three slices of still warm toast from behind my back triumphantly and said,

"Well one of the dogs must've made this toast and put them in the bin then."

Charley agreed that that was indeed the most likely scenario.

It appears I have very gifted Yorkshire Terriers.

Stealing and lying are two of the behaviours which often help Therapeutic Parents to celebrate some of their less than therapeutic moments. The red mist descends with alarming speed if we are tired or taken unawares.

Charley was not allowed to help herself from the fridge as she kept stealing food. Her sandwiches, (which she needed to take to school), were *in* the fridge. As there was also an issue with Charley 'asking for help' I busied myself at my lap top, hoping she would be able to ask me to get her sandwiches out of the fridge.

There was much huffing and sighing. I caught mutterings of 'I am going to starve' and continued waiting patiently for her to ask for help. After 5 minutes, PH walked into the room and I heard Charley say to PH,

"Please can you get my sandwiches from the fridge?"

Before I had a chance to smile at the breakthrough, it was quickly followed with, …"because Mummy is just sitting there doing nothing!" (in an aggressive and rude tone).

Now I know, that as a Therapeutic parent, I should have responded with 'well done for asking for help'. As my Therapeutic Parenting head appeared to have been firmly replaced with my BTM one, I found myself propelled from my chair, incandescent with rage, and standing in front of Charley shouting,

"I'm not 'doing nothing', I am working to pay for *that* bag!" (point) "and *that* jumper!" (point) "and *these* sandwiches!" (throw). At this juncture the sandwiches left my hand and were propelled out of the back door. Charley quickly followed the sandwich with more mutterings, presumably panicking at the thought of losing some food. I closed the door and turned to PH.

"I am so sorry," I said, "I appear to have lost my temper."

PH assured me that he was not surprised and he had also felt enraged at the tone of voice and implications from her criticisms. Being a fairly perfect PH though, the enragement had been secret.

We identified a new trigger and made a mental note not to let her arrow hit the target again on that particular issue.

13 ~~Stealing~~ Reallocating Money

I was very lucky indeed to have the experience of having a child who was extremely gifted in the re-allocating money department.

William began re allocating money quite early on. He started off small, (almost magpie like), by collecting any coins lying around the house. I fixed this one pretty quickly by saying that I had noticed some of my children needed help in leaving money where it was so I had deliberately left money lying around as a test to see what happened. Obviously the stealing stopped instantly. This was because every time he spotted a spare coin William thought, "Ha! I am not falling for that!"

Of course we had not left any money lying around.

He soon moved on to the more ambitious reallocation of funds. I had left £80 out to pay someone, (yes I know very stupid.... I didn't do it again), and realised it had gone missing. I told all the AC to 'freeze'. Luckily they were all in their pyjamas so had limited places to stash the money.

I almost didn't bother asking the AC who had taken it but thought I had better go through the motions anyway. There was no point at all to this, other than being able to say later on, "Well I DID give you the opportunity."

As everyone denied knowing anything, I left them to their (sometimes illuminating) accusations and went straight to William's room to check his money box. Ta-dah! I must have been psychic. There was the £80 sitting carefully in the bottom of his box.

Sometimes it was quite handy being a BTM as I did not feel the need to engage in the soul searching of the 'Why did you do it?' conversations. Fortunately, this turned out to be the right thing to do. I merely replaced the money, ignored the hysterical denials and put in an extra job to 'pay me back' the time I had spent sorting everything out.

William did not stay at this level of stealing for very long... Oh no, he progressed with alarming speed to minor burglary, swiftly followed by crow barring doors open and helping himself to Christmas funds. To be fair, he *did* spend the £700 down the amusement arcade on Christmas Eve, so at least he didn't waste it on Christmas presents I didn't want.

By the time he was in his late teens we had a safe as well as a petty cash box. He smiled engagingly at the camera as he took the petty cash box, to reallocate some of the funds within, to a more deserving cause. Most likely the William Wobbly Cigarette Fund.

Remarkably, even though William always assured us that it was not him who had taken any money, 'reallocation instances' seemed to reduce significantly when he started living independently.

I found it incredibly helpful to be challenged in this way as it gave me absolutely loads of new strategies and ideas to help all the people who come to our training.

You see? Every cloud....

14 Mothers' ~~Horror~~ Day

Once or twice on Mothers' Day my children have breezed smilingly into my bedroom with daffodils picked from the garden, home-made cards (assisted by Granny) and a fairly dodgy looking 'breakfast in bed'. These moments are to be cherished and the cards are safely filed away with last year's offerings and 'I love you Mummy' pictures, (some the physical evidence of an attachment disorder and some not).

When William was 12 he 'forgot' all about Mother's Day. He 'forgot' while his sisters made their cards. He 'forgot' while everyone went to the shops with their pocket money. He even 'forgot' when his sisters gave me their cards with daffodils picked from the garden.

I know he forgot because I asked him.

At the time I felt: Well what did I expect? After all I am not the 'real mum'. I am masquerading as a mother-wolf in real mother-sheep's clothing. He had to find me out sooner or later.

The following year Rosie gave me a wonderful thank you card. In it she wrote, 'Thank you for everything you've done for me, and managed to write 'love Rosie'.

William and Charley both made me a card. Katie had also managed to go out and buy a nice card with Rosie's help. I told the children how happy I was and asked if they would be able to now cease arguing for the day to make this a happy Mothers' Day for all of us. At this point Sophie proudly handed me her card and told me she had managed to 'buy one get one free' so she already had one for next year.

Rosie marshalled the children into going to the florists and contributing to a bunch of flowers. There was (apparently) some bad feeling about who was contributing what. Sophie was particularly annoyed as she had £5 pocket money whereas William only had £1 following a week of untidy (putrid) bedroom. Sophie felt that the contribution should be made fairer and she should get to keep the majority of her money.

I was happily oblivious to this. I had gone over to my mum's with her gift. Katie and Sophie had volunteered to tidy up for me while I was out.

When I returned the house was in the same state with most of the children having quickly sloped off to see friends.

Unfortunately, Rosie noticed me looking upset and went off to remonstrate with all the naughty children. Much crying, screaming and blaming followed. I rallied the troops and suggested we had a 'party tea surprise' for Granny. Rosie volunteered to prepare it, knowing this would give her maximum food tasting opportunities.

By 530pm I was sitting at the 'party tea table' with my mum and all the children. Glumly, I surveyed the blatantly Rosie-prior-sampled party tea, and the death stares being exchanged by the children who had already calculated there would be one piece of pizza extra. Clearly this was a fundamental error and one that I had learned to avoid years earlier.

Katie asked if I had had a nice day. In the interests of world peace, briefly I considered lying and saying how wonderful it had been; unfortunately, I found my BTM mouth was in charge and it was saying,

"No not really. I didn't enjoy the arguing, fighting and sulking, and I was a bit disappointed when you and Sophie ran off to avoid helping tidy up."

My mum then announced that she had 'always hated Mothers' Day.'

I must admit I was thrilled to hear this, as I had assumed that the day was only tricky for parents of traumatised children. I had imagined birth mothers enjoying 1950's style baking and flower arranging with their securely attached children, overwhelmed with gifts and love.

I asked for more details. She told me that every year was a 'let down'. She always hoped that something magical would happen and she would feel appreciated, but every year she ended up feeling more defeated.

I clearly remembered as a child, traipsing round the shops to buy her presents and putting in quite a bit of effort and told her so. "Yes," she said, "but all the arguing and fighting just ruined it every year!"

I had a sneaky feeling my mother was quite enjoying *my* Mothers' Day experience.

15 ~~Ignoring~~ Managing School Conflicts

Earlier on I mentioned how I don't do homework and how much pleasure that has brought to my life. There are other ways a

BTM can deal with the school which also helps to minimise difficulties with the children.

Therapeutic Parents of children with attachment disorder are invariably seen as the evil, cruel one, as the children are also excellent at eliciting sympathetic responses from those around them.

Charley was particularly gifted at this. I was almost proud of her ingenuity. One day I had a call from the school, (the Headmaster no less), to say that he was very sorry to tell me but Charley had been punching a 13-year-old girl and was in serious trouble. By now I had learnt the hard way *not* to get too involved, so I made suitable 'oh dear' noises and, 'Do what you think is best,' etc.

When Charley returned I merely stated that I knew something had happened. (By now you will notice I had become a bit more expert with therapeutic parenting and my bad-temperedness was squashed down inside and hidden from view a bit more).

Naturally Charley did lots of huffing, sighing and stamping about, saying how innocent she was, they always picked on her etc: By now, however, I knew that the school would do what the school wanted to do regardless of my input.

I had also realised that Charley was expert at manipulating people and getting the solution that she wanted. After all, this was the child who had manipulated a whole swathe of teachers into letting her off homework because they believed I was terminally ill.

I didn't feel inclined to have a conversation with the school yet again reminding them of this. I thought I would just sit back and enjoy the show preparing to pick up the pieces; whoever they might belong too. (My money was on the Headmaster frankly).

Sure enough the next day the Headmaster phoned me and his first words were,

"Mrs Naish I have to congratulate you on what a well brought up child Charley is! I have spoken to her about what happened yesterday and she has explained everything to me in a very mature fashion."

At this point I put my phone on speakerphone, mouthing at Patient Husband "You have GOT to hear this; it's going to be a classic!"

The Headmaster went on to say that having listened to Charley's 'very compelling and grown up' response he realised that in fact *he* had been slightly responsible for the incident that had happened the previous day, and as a result, there would be no consequences for Charley because she had been so apologetic and managed to explain to him how he had contributed to the incident.

I *was* going to ask him how he thought he had been responsible for a 16-year-old punching a 13-year-old at the opposite end of the building to him, but thought it best to leave it there.

By now I was crying silently with laughter, so I ended the call and thanked him for his time. Patient Husband shook his head in silent wonder and asked,

"How does she *do* it?"

When Charley came home I looked at her smiled and offered my congratulations. With her big innocent eyes in her wide, lying face she said, "What?"

I answered, "You pulled a blinder there didn't you?"

As she sashayed away, I swear I saw a little triumphant smug smile beginning to form on her lips.

16 Vagrant Dressing

In *'Minimising Drudgery #13'* I gave you some hints on avoiding sewing. This is due to the fact that your child will now enthrall you with new and interesting ways they are able to destroy their clothing. Entire cuffs are chewed off. Large holes mysteriously appear in the centre of jumpers.

When I exclaimed over the new damage, PMs and BMWCs would tell me that their children also damaged their clothes.

No they don't. Not like my children do, not like children with attachment problems do. Traumatised children are on a subconscious mission to destroy everything they touch, see and wear. Please do not tell me that the tiny little fray marks on the elbows and knees that your child has taken six months to achieve are somehow comparable to the chewed necklines and eaten sleeves 'appearing at a jumper near William' most weeks.

Unfortunately, if you team up the jumper-eating child with the BTM who cannot (or will not) sew, you have a recipe for a lot of clothing disintegrating into little puffs in the AC's wake.

I found the way round this was to quickly employ a housekeeper who would do sewing. This only works if you've got some spare cash, if you haven't, you have to teach your children to sew.

A really good way of doing this is to send them to Army Cadets. Granted they can't join until they are about 12 years old and it quite a long time to wait for repairs, *but* at least once they get there, they are actually taught to sew their badges on. From then on you can say (with some validation), that you are teaching your children independence skills and they do all their own sewing- so "Sorry if it's a bit of a mess but don't criticise it because it will only hurt their feelings. They have done their *best*."

Smile fondly and withdraw.

I did not discover 'Chewelry' and other helpful aids until my children were too old to benefit. On the plus side this meant when they left home, there was less to pack.

My AC became very attached to the same item of clothing; wearing it over and over. All these things combined to ensure that they often walked round looking like a load of vagrants. This was not helped by the un-matching grubby socks. Of course I did challenge this and did quite a lot of, "That's alright I will rest here until you are ready," etc. But this is much easier in theory than in practice.

Sophie (Spikey) surpassed herself in the 'vagrant dressing department', but did so by concealing the vagrancy in her little Sophie sneaky way. *(See Sophie Spikey Has a Very Big Problem, Sarah Naish and Rosie Jefferies, Jessica Kingsley Publishing October 2016).*

On one occasion as we were shopping in town, I noticed that Sophie was walking strangely. I saw that the shoes she was wearing were in fact her old ones which I had put in the bin some days previously. I asked Sophie why she was 'walking funny', and her mottled face told me all I needed to know.

I said I needed to look at her shoe to check it was fitting okay and then quickly picked her foot up to look at the bottom. At first I thought I was hallucinating as there was no bottom to the shoe. All I could see was Sophie's formerly white (ish) sock, now black, with the shell of the shoe over the top. At this stage in my therapeutic parenting journey I knew that the question 'why' was no longer part of my vocabulary and would only result in more bad-temperedness for me, and provide a plethora of mad lying opportunities for her.

We quickly decamped for hot chocolate and a little bit of 'wondering aloud' which made us all feel better. I also got to eat a fair amount of cake to help lower my cortisol levels.

17 Hysterical 'Playfulness'

Happy news! The therapeutic parenting term 'Playfulness' can easily be transformed into *you* having a jolly nice time!

Therapeutic Parents use 'Playfulness to help 'flip' their AC from defiance and the inevitable descent into rudeness/ aggression, for example when they:

- Refuse to get dressed

- Insist on wearing appalling half-eaten clothing

- Lie on the floor of the supermarket at crucial movement time

The *idea* is to quickly engage in some light-hearted playful distraction which defuses the situation, (something most BTMs struggle with to be honest).

So for example if your AC is about to smash the computer because the printer 'won't work' and you discover a spoon thoughtfully wedged inside the printer, a playful response would be;

"What an excellent idea! I will just go and get the rest of the cutlery to put there too!"

It's very easy to get carried away with playfulness though and it swiftly becomes more therapeutic for the BTM than the child.

When William (aged 15) screamed at me that I was 'not right in the head' and engaged in an out-of-control smashing session, I thoughtfully went and put on my favourite neon orange wellies and my rescued purple pac-a-mac, I then presented myself before him with a flourish as a fashionista.

Smashing noises stopped and were replaced with incredulous muttered gasps of "What the hell are you *doing*?"

"Well I thought about what you said William, about me not being 'right in the head'. I think you may have a point!"

He tried very hard not to smile, but failed.

Once everything had calmed down, really I should have just gone and got changed. But no. By then I was having such a thoroughly enjoyable time that I decided to do an entire fashion show, mixing together my favourite neons and pouting on an imaginary catwalk.

When PH returned home he took in the trashed room, glazed looks of boredom on the children's faces, and me, dressed up in un-matching neons, strutting up and down the lounge to Madonna's 'Vogue' and quickly put the kettle on.

He had learnt by then not to try to solve the problems or enquire as to how my day had been.

The children also learnt very quickly not to call me a 'fat cow', as 'fat cows' had a tendency to drag themselves about on the floor, mooing quite a lot.

My favourite 'playfulness' which to be honest was more about me enjoying myself, was when taking the children shopping. If there was some dysregulated behaviour I would begin singing, quite softly at first. If the behaviour continued the volume would increase to a point where I would be shouting 'Land of Hope and Glory' with accompanying conductor arm movements. By the time they were all teens, I used to hear them whispering to each other "Do *not* tell her not to sing, she will just sing louder!"

#18 ~~Stalking~~ Following

Social workers call it 'following', Therapeutic Parents call it 'stalking' - One of the problems that I encountered very early on was one I termed 'stalking'. This makes an already stressed BTM feel like she might actually suffocate and die. Most of my five children were dedicated 'stalkers'.

As there was more than one child they developed a 'holding pattern' of stalking. One child was 'primary stalker' while the next one either waited patiently, watching out of the corner of their eye for a bit of a stalking opportunity, or started competing with the stalker elect, intending to distract him.

Sometimes the stalking was subtle. The child leant on me, and this was initially taken to be a genuine sign of affection. Then I noticed the child was ALWAYS leaning on me! I couldn't actually sit down without the child being sucked into my side like I had developed invisible hoovering skills.

I had become a 'stalkee'.

Then I noticed how difficult it was 'to get up these days'. One child was on my lap, one sucked into my right side, one to my left... oh and who was this lying on my feet, gazing up at me adoringly?

The problem was, that when I tried to explain it to a Patronising Professional it sounded a bit lame really. They looked at the blatantly BTM and heard,

'Sophie keeps following me about'. Or

'William is overly affectionate'.

The Patronising Professional may sometimes say:

- "Aah bless, he is a bit insecure

- Isn't it great that he feels secure enough with you to show his affection? This means he isn't attachment disordered!

- Have you tried reassuring him?"

(Imaginary punch)

This causes great unease for the BTM, as they know that the stalking is <u>not</u> affection, although at first they may have believed it was a positive sign. The full horror of being stalked 24 hours a day, 7 days a week, by more than one child is very difficult to put into words. You come out of the toilet. He's there. Beaming at you. (He was already banging on the door anyway the whole time you were in the toilet). You go to the kitchen. She trots along behind you clinging to your skirt or even wrapping herself around your leg which makes walking challenging. The other child wraps themselves round your other leg. Goodness... they really love their Mummy. Silent screaming bursts out into a merry sounding opera song.

This is GOOD. It reduces your cortisol levels.

#19 Assisting IRTs to Leave Home

When IRT, Rosie Rudey, turned 16, this meant several things to her:

- She knew everything

- What she didn't know wasn't worth knowing

- I was a vacuous idiot with no knowledge of anything relevant to her life

- She was, in fact, in charge of the world

- Everything I had learned about paying bills etc. did not apply to her as she was a 'supreme being'.

She was going to move out on the basis that her brother and sisters were 'so annoying'. I observed that she found the others 'so annoying' because they would not do as she said. She often insulted them and spoke in a rude and disparaging way to them. She then quickly became outraged when they answered her back.

I have no idea where she had picked up these bad-tempered ways.

Rosie was surprised that I was encouraging her to move out. I pointed out how much it costs to live in a bed-sit, but she was convinced that she could manage on her education allowance (£30pw) and her Saturday job (£34pw). This would give her ample money to live, buy clothes and furniture, pay her huge mobile phone costs, eat, socialise, travel to and from college and probably run a modest yacht.

I explained that she would also need money for a rental deposit, a month in advance, water, gas, electricity and rates. Rosie looked at me (mockingly) and declared that I really should 'get a life'. I decided it was my moral duty to assist her in getting her own.

She underestimated my delight at the prospect of her moving out. There was hope in my heart of a house where there was less tension, less anger, less punching and less IRTs.

Unfortunately, she (naturally) lost her job when she decided that it was 'too rainy' to go to the (cosy, indoor) shop one Saturday. She was livid when the boss promptly sacked her. Apparently it was 'so unfair', and the boss had 'such a bad attitude'. I pointed out to Rosie that there were about 30,000 unemployed 16-year-olds locally, who would quite like to work and get paid. She was unimpressed and accused me of 'making problems'.

I half-jokingly offered to make her homeless and she seized on this idea with delight, informing me she could claim housing benefit. She had 'looked into it' apparently and 'loads of her friends' had done it. Her eyes lit up at the prospect of being kicked out of her home so that she could loll about in bed on a Saturday, (thereby making it indistinguishable from all the other days of the week).

One month later, she was living in a bed and breakfast. She was puzzled that her £30 per week income support did not stretch very far when one's diet consisted entirely of 'pot noodles'. She had lost her education allowance after giving up college on the basis that it was 'too boring'.

The Government (much to my fury) were kindly paying her rent and giving her £30 a week so she could get drunk with her friends.

Patient Husband and I were summoned by Rosie in a late night phone call, informing us that 'everything had gone wrong'. When we went to scrape Rosie up off the floor outside the kebab shop, she looked at me and said,

"Don't tell my Mum will you?"

I reminded Rosie that I was indeed her mother.

Rosie said, "No you don't unnershtand, she will KILL me!"

Patient Husband and I suppressed our mirth and drove Rosie back home. We spent the next day clattering pots and pans, playing loud music and asking her if she felt ok.

She agreed breezily that she felt absolutely fine, through clenched teeth in a white, sweaty face.

Her return home was a pleasant affair for all concerned. Gone was the IRT. In her place was someone we all rather liked: Even if there were occasional flashes of bad-temperedness which Patient Husband said reminded him of someone.....

PART FOUR:

EVERYTHING ELSE ANNOYS ME TOO

NOW!

Over the years I have found that my bad-temperedness has extended its tentacles from the Arguing Children, Perfect Mothers and Patronising Professionals to just about everything else. I can hardly walk down the road some days without thinking a scathing thought, which I instantly try (usually unsuccessfully) to correct.

I know NOW that compassion fatigue when caring for traumatised children plays a major part in exhaustion, disengagement and general feelings of dissatisfaction, but I didn't know that THEN- not when I was in the middle of it, letting my entire chocolate-augmented body hang by the broken fally-off bits of my nails.

I have no idea how PH managed to stay patient during those times when everything annoyed me. My fuse became so short it was invisible.

Even though the compassion fatigue has rescinded now, (remarkably it seemed to diminish directly in proportion to numbers of children leaving home), I still have left-over bad-temperedness, which is so entrenched that it appears to have become part of my personality.

Here are some of the other things which have ensured I remained a dedicated Bad-Tempered-Mother, even in the absence of Arguing Children.

Annoying Thing #1 - 4x4s

BTMs normally like 4x4s because generally, they are not very PC and BTMs can have satisfying arguments about them.

When the children were younger I *had* to have a 7 seater 4x4 but I did not like it. I mourned every day for my lovely convertible BMW. I had to part exchange the BMW for the wretched 4x4 because (apparently):

- We lived in the country
- I suddenly had 5 children
- We couldn't physically get out of the drive in the winter
- I got trapped in the forest when it snowed
- We had 7 dogs
- We had 2 goats who sometimes have to go to the vets.
- Our county floods very badly and sometimes only 4x4s can get about.

I didn't care about all of this. Patient Husband did though, and he kept being sensible and annoyingly right. I worried that I was being likened to the tidy-hair-mummies in Kensington who wear sunglasses to drive their enormous Range Rovers through the dry, paved streets in heavy traffic.

I liked driving about in my BMW with the hood down even when it was cold. It made me stop feeling bad-tempered. When 2 of the

AC were sitting in the back, I could put the music up really loud and not hear them. Naturally they couldn't manage the uncertainty-lottery about whose turn it was to actually get to *go* in the BMW, so when we got the 4x4 we quickly learned that the best way to stop my ears bleeding was to:

- Allocate each child a particular spot which NEVER changed

- Leave something of theirs in their space so that Sophie Spikey couldn't pretend she had forgotten, and accidentally sit in William's cherished seat

- Develop deafness when Rosie Rudey launched her 'Rights to sit in front seat' manifesto

Every day when I drove about, my only consolation was knowing that I had a powerful stereo and that I was contributing to global warming, so hopefully we would have a nice summer soon.

Annoying Thing # 2 – Pointless Fluorescent Jackets

On the way to school, I used to always see a woman with 3 small children. For 8 years she had 3 small children. I don't understand this. Why didn't they grow?

She was quite clearly a Baking-Mother-With-Clipboard and put fluorescent jackets on her small children, to walk up the two inch car- free lane to school. As a BTM I found this unacceptable. I know she was only doing it to wind me up and to make the point that she was a BMWC. I felt she enjoyed feeling superior to all the BTMs whose children (ie. mine), were walking to school, across fields, unaccompanied, fluorescent jacket-less, blatantly wearing unmatched socks.

Every day I had to control the urge to swerve a bit too close to the little crowd of fluorescent jackets, just so I could say, "Sorry I did not see you!"

I know she would have told me that they were wearing the jackets as it was a 'Health and Safety EU Directive.' I bet she would have been able to quote the paragraph number and subsection. That just made me want to swerve a bit more.

Only slightly more annoying than pointless fluorescent jackets, were the accompanying pointless hard hats worn by important looking men in suits. Normally they were gazing into a hole on a side street and scratching their chins, holding clipboards and arguing. In these circumstances, they only *needed* a hard hat in case a BTM comes along and whacked them.

When I am driving around now, I am often fortuitous enough to see more pointless fluorescent jackets worn by men in hard-hats on permanent tea breaks. They are always several metres from any pseudo roadworks, carefully coned off by purposeless cones, presumably only there for a 'cone-vention' as no work whatsoever is happening. The only thing working is the traffic lights, carefully phased to let 3 cars through at a time.

My children now all seem to remark on pointless cones and fluorescent jackets. Sometimes we can even have a happy little blame fest as we drive along.

Annoying Thing #3 ~~Idiot~~ Cold Call Phone Calls

Recently I attended a business meeting with a colleague. Shortly afterwards, my phone rang and the conversation went like this:

Me: "Sarah Naish speaking"

Caller: "Can I speak to Mrs Sarra Neesh"

Me: (loudly, already bad-tempered), "Sarah NAISH-PRONOUNCED NAYSHE - SPEAKING!"

Caller: "Lovely to speak to you, I am phoning from Accident care line/ claim PPI now/ Insurance Survey inc" (I didn't listen to where they were calling from) "How are you today?"

Me: (Taking a leaf out of Rosie Rudey's book)- "What do you want?"

Caller: "Mrs Neesh I am phoning about your recent accident…"

Me: "You mean the one I had 2 minutes ago? Wow that is fast!"

Caller: "Um yes I think it is about that one. I am phoning to tell you about compensation you are due….."

Me: "This is excellent news. You mean because I 'accidentally' picked up the phone to yet another moronic cold-calling company, when I have specifically blocked my number from this type of call that you are giving me compensation? Good. About time too. How much are you paying me?"

Caller: "No Mrs Neesh, you misunderstand me….."

Me: "Goodbye" (ends call, blocks number).

My colleague was staring at me open mouthed, she said she always ended up getting into lengthy conversations with cold callers because she 'did not want to hurt their feelings.' I explained that a much quicker way is to simply place the phone on the table, leave the person speaking, and go off to have a cup of tea or walk round the garden.

This is one of the absolute benefits of Therapeutic Parenting. You simply DO NOT HAVE TIME for this kind of vacuous nonsense, so it's really easy for us to cut to the chase and airbrush these annoyances out of our lives, swiftly and effectively.

I apologise for all the people working in call centres..... But not very profusely.

Annoying Thing #4 Family Pets

The Therapeutic Parent wonders why some people prefer children to pets. She finds this a very strange idea.

The reason we had seven dogs and five children is because dogs produce oxytocin. This means that a BTM can actually get a 'feel good' factor from her dogs which she cannot get from her children. (Incidentally the AC also benefit hugely from the oxytocin production).

Every time we go training and I explain about dogs and oxytocin I can guarantee that someone will also ask about cats. NO! Cats do not produce oxytocin in people. They are takers, dogs are givers. I didn't make this up, there is research and everything.

Once I bought two rabbits to keep the goats company. Charley Chatty cackled with laughter when the goats head-butted the rabbits so they 'flew'. I had to change things round a bit:

My father, who was not an animal lover at all, (but did have three children), said he did not understand why I had all these animals and asked me what the 'point' was. I replied,

"When I get home, the dogs gather excitedly at the gate. They wag their tails and are clearly thrilled to see me. They don't ask anything of me, yet are always grateful for what I give them. The goats bleat for their breakfast. The children bleat for breakfast, dinner, tea, snacks, pocket money, sweets and my constant undivided attention. The rabbits are silent and happy to keep our grass short," (apart from short goat-instigated flights). My father nodded and agreed I should probably get another dog or rabbit.

When the BTM thinks about 'family pets' they think initially that it will be 'nice for the children' to have 'something else to do'. IE something other than arguing or moaning. Unfortunately, now we need to add to the daily chores of getting the children up, dressed, breakfasted and off to school, the tasks of;

- cleaning out the rabbit,

- walking/training the dog,

- feeding the guinea pig,

- stopping the goats from bullying the rabbits,

- taking them to the vets,

- letting the goats out,

- stopping them fighting,

- getting the mice out of the goats' food,

- getting drowned mice out of the goats' water

- making sure the rabbits water hasn't frozen overnight etc.

....will all obviously be her new job to fit into her 'spare time'.

My little 'literal Lilly' (Sophie Spikey), used to have to move her guinea pigs every morning so they had fresh grass. One day I suggested that she went out and moved them in the evening to save her some time in the morning. After five minutes she came rushing back in in a panic, "Mummy, Mummy! The guinea pigs are eating tomorrow's grass!"

I suggested she went out and put a notice up saying, 'Do not eat the grass.' She looked puzzled, "But Mummy guinea pigs can't read."

We stupidly bought some baby goats. I thought the goats would be lovely sweet pets. I forgot that as I am a Bad-Tempered Mother I also have bad-tempered children. This meant that Charley Chatty, briefly in competition with Rosie Rudey, thought it was a good idea to be the 'boss of the goats' and shout and scream at them at regular intervals. Even though I did my best to model better behaviour it did not seem to work....(too little too late I suspect).

The cute little baby kids which we had brought home from the farm quickly turned into very bad-tempered head-butting nasty evil-staring full-size goats. I had to rehome them (briefly) when they nearly broke Charley's leg in revenge. On the plus side they did cause the children and passersby some hilarity when they managed to get on the roof of the house, running about and playing a lovely game. I did not find it hilarious.

We used to have a trampoline for the children. This probably made me look like a Good or Perfect Mother, making sure my children had lovely toys to entertain themselves with. Actually it was in order to help the children to get rid of excess energy after school. By then I knew about cortisol levels and how trampolines help to lower the levels and help children to regulate so that was all the excuse I needed.

It all went a bit wrong on the day the goats also got on the trampoline with the children. Standing on the balcony taking amusing photos of the two goats bouncing happily alongside my eight and 10-year-old, I suddenly realised that if there was an accident, A&E would never believe my story.

"Yes, I am sorry the deep gouges in my child's stomach are from the goats playing on the trampoline with them."

Yeah right.

Annoying Thing #5 Political Correctness

During a fostering or adoption assessment, naturally foster parents and adopters pretend to be VERY PC as they are dealing with Social Workers. This fades quickly once the parent is faced with decisions made by Patronising Professionals, based in political correctness which puts their child's well-being at risk. Decisions like;

- You have to take out a mobile contract in your own name for your 17-year-old son to promote his 'independence'. You protest he has an emotional and functioning age of 5 but that is of no consequence.

- We must always believe the child. Even when what they are saying is blatantly a lie and is actually confusing the child and deepening their trauma because idiots are listening to them.

- You must allow your indiscriminately affectionate 7-year-old to hug any visitor.

My best/worst example of political correctness gone mad is this story.

One day my daughter, then aged seven, was told by her school that she was not allowed to wear a tankini for her swimming lessons. Now for those of you who have never had the need to buy or wear a tankini, I should explain that it is a swimming garment which looks much like a full swimming costume, with a long top and high pants, no gap in the middle.

As a committed 'BTM/ Therapeutic Parent against nonsense rules', I told my daughter's school that the tankini rule was a *Very Silly Rule*. The school (who were a little bit scared of me), told me that indeed they agreed and they also thought it was a Very Silly Rule, but that the swimming pool had insisted on this rule.

Undeterred, I drove purposefully down to the swimming pool and enquired of the 12-year-old gum-chewing receptionist as to why my daughter was unable to wear her (new) tankini for her swimming lessons. The helpful assistant told me that it was 'The Rule'.

Sensing that I was dealing with an Incredibly Rude Teenager, cunningly disguised as a Helpful Assistant, I asked to speak to 'The Manager'.

The Manager was not in, so the 18-year-old Assistant Manager came out to 'help'. I explained the query once more.

The Assistant Manager clarified that children were not allowed to wear tankinis because of 'Child Protection Issues'.

It was very unfortunate for the Assistant Manager that I was in fact a BTM AND former social worker, who knew a great deal about 'Child Protection' and abhorred all forms of political correctness gone mad.

The hapless Assistant Manager did not realise that she had put the match of ignorance to the anti PC bonfire.

I asked the unsuspecting Assistant Manager which part of the Child Protection Procedures or Children Act, the 'wearing of a tankini' contravened. The Assistant Manager (panicking somewhat) suggested that the child might dive into the water and the bottoms could come down, thereby exposing the child's bum to the lurking paedophile, so stupidly invited to the (closed pool) school swimming lessons.

Gasping in pretend horror, I enquired as to what steps the leisure centre were taking to ensure boys were not put at risk in the same way when diving in with swimming trunks on, with NO top on even. The Assistant Manager became very confused and reiterated that it was 'The Rule'. She then went on to say, (quite frantically) that perhaps the child could become entangled in the tankini straps and die.

I smirked a bit at this and tried to imagine a scenario where this could possibly happen. "In 30 years of child care,' I told the Assistant Manager, 'I have never heard of a child being murdered by their own swimming costume."

I suggested (quite politely for me) that perhaps the Assistant Manager could get a grown up to check the law and Child Protection Procedures. I further suggested that the world would be a much nicer place for children if some of the hysteria surrounding tankinis and similar PC mad rules could be dispensed with.

I made sure my daughter wore her tankini to swimming the following week. Luckily she did not report any sexual predator lurking nearby, nor did she become entangled in the straps and die.

I do not need to be told that a heat gun from B&Q is 'not to be used as a hairdryer'. Tempting though it may be at times, to use it as one on my Arguing Children's wet heads.

Nor do I need reminding that the contents of the coffee cup I bought 'may be hot'. If it were not hot, I would take it back and be very bad- tempered about it.

We wonder why we cannot say 'black' anymore. Black is a colour like 'red'. BTM's will not allow their children to sing 'Baa Baa Rainbow Sheep', when there are black and white sheep clearly frolicking in the adjacent field.

When I was working as a Social Worker, in my office I blatantly asked for black or white coffee instead of coffee 'with' or coffee 'without'. I took great delight in watching my social work colleagues blanch in horror.

My black friends speak unashamedly about 'blackboards' not chalkboards and 'blackbirds' apparently without fear. They tell me they do this deliberately to confuse people.

Annoying Thing #6 Teens Walking Insolently in the Road

BTMs get *really* bad-tempered when they are taking the children to school and they are faced with swathes of rude, insolent teenagers sauntering out nonchalantly in front of their cars staring at them and daring them to hit them.

I found this particularly trying and was very tempted to keep my foot on the accelerator and make sure that I ploughed through the centre. I realised as a professional working with children this may not be good for my career. My children also felt this was unreasonable.

I had to settle for merely narrowly missing them with my wing mirror as I breezed on past. Mind you, this did make sure that they recognised my car pretty swiftly and got out of the way. My children later told me that I was known locally as 'the mad lady' who would actually get out of her car and take issue with them, shouting and screaming in her orange wellies and purple pac-a-mac.

Now, I often drive over the common and see the cows and sheep munching grass at the side of the road. Frequently, the sheep especially, will gaze at me approaching and then amble quickly and deliberately into the centre of the road where they regard me haughtily. I am always reminded of the same vacant stares of the teenagers sauntering in front of my car. The only difference is that the sheep are not looking at their phones, or wearing headphones....

Annoying Thing #7 Coffee mornings & small-talk

In 'Dealing with Annoying People' (Part One), I explained how to get rid of people who pop in (#8 and #10). Therapeutic Parents who have become BTMs are extremely bad at coffee mornings and socialising. This is because coffee mornings contain small-talk. Bad-tempered mothers do not do small-talk, it is akin to baking. The dedicated BTM knows that people who do baking also make small-talk. This means that if you should be unwise enough to have a coffee morning or even *attend* a coffee morning, you are destined to be surrounded by PMs twittering on about:

- baking,

- cupcakes,

- nappies,

- the birth,

- their child's achievements,

- the best type of flower to put in bedding in the shade,

- the new council initiative for recycling and what it all means....

If ever I was unlucky enough to have to attend a social event containing small talk I would spend the majority of my time in the toilet or outside in the garden. Luckily I don't get invited to very many places anymore.

Therapeutic Parents want to talk about more important things like how to stop their son weeing in the pot plants, or what to do about their daughter absconding in the night.

BTMs do not want to talk about anything. They are past caring.

One of the additional horrors faced by adopters and foster parents is the well-meant but ill-conceived organised 'Carers coffee mornings'. When we did our research into compassion fatigue in fostering, *(University of Bristol and Fostering Attachments Ltd November 2016)* we found that most carers had had negative experiences with coffee mornings. We have heard similar stories at our training events. Carers complained about:

- Staff being always present and advising what could and couldn't be discussed

- Not being allowed to mention the children they were looking after

- Not being allowed to discuss what happened in other agencies

- Not being allowed to say anything negative about the staff

- Being told to bring the coffee and cakes themselves

- Being told it was compulsory

- Having to listen in silence to 'Guest Speakers' who didn't seem to know what they were talking about.

So that sounded like real fun!

Naturally being pretty feisty Therapeutic Parents, with a very good sprinkling of BTMs, the carers (in the main), merely decamped and set up their own beautiful whinge-fest, where they could talk about what they wanted and consume copious amounts of coffee and alcohol. Everyone left feeling much better.

Annoying Thing #8 Letters from School

If I had 5p for every letter home while my children were at school, I would have been able to pay my mortgage off. What is the point of them? I was not interested in book fairs and non-uniform days. I am a Therapeutic Parent. School was respite. If the children happened to learn something there at the same time, then that was really lucky because that would help them to leave home much more quickly.

Letters home from school serve three purposes

1. to remind me of things but I had already decided were not important enough to remember

2. to castigate me

3. to ask me to help them to do something which nobody else wanted to do.

The only letters the Therapeutic Parent does not receive at all, are the really critical ones. These are the letters telling you that you *must* return the letter by tomorrow at the latest if you want to remove your child from your house on a fantastic school trip, for *five whole days*. These letters always stayed at the bottom of my child's bag.

I would receive letters which only needed to go directly into the bin. Ones about;

- last week's school fete,
- the new (nonsensical) behaviour management strategy,
- the 'Guide to helping your child with their homework' and
- the famous annual 'Parents Open Evening appointments' (one day too late)
- Suggestions for a nice healthy packed lunch.

Annoying Thing #9 Personalised number plates

The true Therapeutic Parent does not have time to notice number plates. Any number plates. Or even cars really.

The BTM *does* notice number plates. They stand out like annoying, taunting little beacons. She has no idea why anyone would want to put personalised number plates on their car. It is not because she has a particularly horrible or cheap car, she may not even drive. The BTM just *knows* that people who drive cars with personalised number plates are basically people who are going to annoy her.

The BTM thinks she would probably spend the £33,000 it cost to do a very clever anagram of someone's boring name, on ice cream, chocolate or indeed a car that did not stall every time she got to the traffic lights. Preferably one with a glass partition between herself and the AC.

I am sorry if you have one, but seriously what is the point of them? You might as well just have a car sticker saying, 'I was going to get a personalised number plate but sponsored a child in Africa instead'. Everyone will have more respect for you and know that you are not the kind of person to try and show off or make jokes, which frankly don't work.

I know I am coming across as bitter, but I thought it only fair to warn you. As a BTM I will be more bad-tempered if you pop round to see me in a car with personalised number plates. Go and spend the money on the third world debt, and get a nice little letter every Christmas from a child in Africa instead.

Annoying Thing #10 Weekends Do Not Exist

When I first realised but I would need to go back to work as well as looking after my children I felt dismay. On my first day back at work however, I suddenly found myself free to eat lunch unencumbered, in blissful silence and with both hands. Very quickly I learnt to appreciate the freedom of going to work which was *always* without fail, 1000 times easier than any day I spent at home being a full-time Therapeutic Parent.

Straightaway I challenged my Patient Husband about the being-tired-after-work lie.

Naturally there also still remained the same amount of house work and 'AC need' left over from the day, but this was carefully and considerately saved up for me to return to in the evening.

On the Friday there was a marked difference when people were leaving work. Some people would skip to their cars looking forward to nights out, bottles of wine and a relaxing weekend. Perfect Mothers would leave exactly on time carrying freshly baked bread and armfuls of flowers, purchased in a busy lunch break, ready to do a special dinner that evening. Good Mothers were on their way off to an upbeat family gathering with the in-laws.

The other BTMs loitered with me. Anything to put off that Friday feeling. No not *that* Friday feeling, the one that BTMs and every Therapeutic Parent has. Our Friday feeling is something like, 'Once more unto the breach dear friends.' Coupled with a quick, 'Help me God to get through to Monday morning.'

Later in my Therapeutic Parenting 'additional skills' training, I rapidly implemented a strategy to help keep me sane and increase my chocolate eating opportunities. By simply adding on an hour to my working day I left at the usual time but then parked up in the nearest Starbucks on my way back to have a nice little treat.

This enabled me to face my AC with a smile on my face, briefly at least.

Annoying Thing #11 Super-Mum Says 'Shut Up'

When people discover I have adopted five children who are all siblings, I generally face three different responses.

- They look at me aghast

- They start talking about a child they sponsor in Africa as if it is in some way comparable

- They say 'Aren't you wonderful'? Or 'good' or 'amazing'

It is this last response which is guaranteed to make me want to leave quickly.

No, I am not 'good', or 'wonderful' or 'amazing'. I am someone who selfishly wanted to have children. All adoptions start because the adopters want to meet their own need of becoming a parent. As an adopter, I didn't want to be patronised, I just wanted to get on with parenting my children.

Over the years, I found the media work I did, ended up in the same old place. It didn't matter if I had met the reporter to talk about

- Important ground breaking research

- Successful training,

- A new book release,

- The amount of time the water company were taking to fill in a trench in my garden-

-The interviewers would quickly get the subject round to the 'wonderful' and 'heartwarming' story of how I had 'taken in' my five children (as if they were bedraggled puppies) and 'offered them a home.'

I was uncooperative and insisted on keeping them on topic which led to much disappointment and persistent questioning.

In one memorable radio interview where Rosie and I were talking about compassion fatigue in foster care, the interviewer suddenly asked Rosie if she was 'grateful' to me for 'taking her in'. I almost saw the old 'Rudey' part attempting a brief coup, and after a brief sigh she asked the reporter what they meant. I swiftly interrupted and said I thought gratitude was an interesting misconception, giving Rosie time to use her own pointy- eyebrow-death-stare which seemed to stop further misguided questioning.

At the end of the interview the reporter would always turn to me, syrup like, and ask what advice I had for other adopters and foster carers thinking of doing the same. They wanted me to say,

"I highly recommend it. It's a wonderful life." Instead I disappointed them with a realistic answer,

"I would tell them to read everything they can on developmental trauma and attachment, oh and buy all the furniture from Ikea." It didn't matter how they phrased it, I would not sugar coat it.

There was often frustrated sighing.

Annoying Thing #12 Sport

All of it. All sport. From the Olympics appearing on the TV with alarming regularity, to hysteria over how we might qualify for some pointless trophy, to watching AC not join in sports day.

The lot.

PART FIVE:

HOLIDAYS ARE <u>NOT</u> A REST

Fact #1 A Holiday Isn't a Holiday

During the first year my children lived with me I made the famous and fatal novice error of trying to 'go on holiday'. We make this mistake because we are exhausted, disillusioned and often overwhelmed. In a previous life when we felt like this we would 'have a break'. What I had entirely failed to take into consideration, was that now my 'break' would have the cause of my *need* for a break, coming with me.

Happily oblivious, off we trundled to Center Parks in November. What could go wrong?... They had an indoor swimming pool, family friendly restaurants and lodges in the trees. It was going to be a wonderful family holiday. As it was the early days I had failed to take into consideration the fact that my children had suffered early life trauma, and therefore even a local trip to the nearest park would be a source of hysterical acting out.

At the time I was not with Patient Husband, I was with Lazy Husband. I should have realised that a trip to a holiday park with several very young children and a lazy husband could not end well.

Sure enough, on the first day when I needed to take them swimming, LH had 'important football' to watch on the television.

Undeterred I marched off through the woods with three small children, aged 8 months, 2 and 3, all wearing nappies. (Not me - although at times it would have been easier).

In the changing room it was like a scene from groundhog day. It seemed that the more I undressed one, the more another put their clothes back on. I quickly learnt to multitask and make efficient use of pushchair straps and playpens.

Upon entering the swimming pool with three costume clad children (complete with swim nappies), I noticed that as a toe touched the water William pooed himself.

We all went back to the changing room and toilets, with me muttering and swearing under my breath, (in French so the children did not learn the bad words).

Once William was changed we went back to the water only to find that in all the excitement Sophie had also pooed herself. As we all trudged back to the changing room's, with Charley screaming and Sophie blotchy and stressed, I formed the idea for a book with a section in about not planning happy days out

Twenty minutes later we were again ready to enter the children's swimming pool. Once we got up to our ankles I was approached by a lifeguard. He was clearly a very important man.

He told me I was not allowed to have three children. I did not know what he meant as I had clearly been approved by the adoption panel, my first three children had been placed with me and here we all were. I told him so. I had letters.

"No," he said, "you can't have three children in the swimming pool." I asked him where he would like me to put them and he replied,

"No you can't have three children with only one person." I informed him I was a single parent with three children, (because it did feel that way to be honest), but he just repeated that I still 'could not come in with the three children.'

Now, at this stage of my Therapeutic Parenting journey, I was a newbie. Later on as a Therapeutic Parent with enhanced BTM capabilities, faced with the same situation again - I would simply have continued and dared them to try to manhandle us all out- or I would have asked them to call the police. Unfortunately, at this point I was blissfully unaware that we were going to have to fight for everything we ever needed. I thought it was a one off.

An hour later, we were all trudging back to the holiday lodge through the park. It was at this point that it started snowing. Shortly afterwards Sophie fell over and badly grazed both knees and her face. With visions of the Child-Protection-Police bearing down on me, I swapped a crying Sophie over with Charley in the pushchair and carried Charley, (who was already a fairly hefty lump). William traipsed silently alongside, no doubt wondering what on earth was going on, and missing his old foster carer.

On our return to the lodge LH was having a lovely time finishing up watching the football. We walked in covered in snow and blood having not even achieved the swimming. "Have a nice time?" he asked.

We didn't stay together very long after that.

This little 'mini-non-break' also included highlights such as increases in bedwetting, nightmares, and William attempting to climb out the window during his sleep. I learnt that holidays were no longer 'breaks'. Holidays were 'experiences' for the BTM to endure, and for the children to hopefully get through, without increasing their trauma.

Fact #2 The Journey Out Will Be Stressful

My favourite 'hysterical playfulness' tactic, came to the fore whilst travelling outbound on holiday. At times of maximum dysregulation, I would merely lie down on the airport floor. This made the children gather around me and interrupted the drama and arguing for a few minutes. I did not pretend to be unconscious, although this was an attractive idea.

It is a stupid idea to take children, who can't manage transitions on any holiday. It is even more of a stupid idea to bring them into contact with authoritative foreigners who don't see the 'funny side' of 'joking about bombs'.

It is also, a very bad idea for BTMs to go to any country with less than friendly immigration or security measures in place. The BTM is likely to become much more bad-tempered even more quickly. It is difficult enough to get several children through passport control and security. The BTM's children make going through security even more tricky than it already is. The IRT will decide that she doesn't know that 'liquid foundation is liquid', and therefore has to go through security in a clear plastic bag. She will keep it in her make-up bag and then be surprised, hurt, shocked, and upset when the security man throws it away. A tantrum ensues.

Although it is very difficult getting through the airport and on to the plane, all the difficulties faced by the BTM during transit, pale into insignificance when faced with the might of American immigration. The BTM is often heard to refer to the might of American Immigration as 'those wankers'.

Whilst queuing to get into America, (often at risk of missing the connecting flight), several BTMs can be heard commenting on the unhelpfulness of American officials. They might say;

- "Why do they think we would want to stay in their country?

- But I am happy in England!

- We will miss our bloody flight!

- Did they not know an airplane was landing and that they would need more than two important men with miserable faces to deal with 1000 people?

- I can't believe they're making us queue to get *in* to the country."

Be warned. The AC will happily join in such treason and have NO inhibitors. Step away.

Fact #3 The AC Will Be Resistant to 'Other Cultures'

The BTM struggles to stop her children pointing and laughing at the very heavily laden electronic wheelchairs. She can be heard muttering under her breath, as she approaches yet another lardilly challenged individual, ladled into a wheelchair, built in the shape of a small forklift truck.

In Florida, unfortunately I had my work cut out in relation to 'fat acceptance' if I am honest. I would say to the children, "Don't look, don't stare, don't point."

The children looked, stared and pointed. They could not believe that the squeaking wheelchair could possibly manage to continue moving, with the half ton of human detritus spilling out on all sides. Naturally, Rosie Rudey loudly said unhelpful things like, "God they should make fat people walk, that way they'd lose some weight!"

In Spain, Sophie Spikey launched her campaign of 'only eating beige food'.

In Greece, having accidentally settled down on a nudist beach, the children had a mixture of reactions to a naked, saggy elderly couple walking past. This included;

- Shrieks of horror and rushing to me for comfort

- Pointing and laughing with fake falling over in hysterics

- Stunned expressions of revulsion and "Old people shouldn't be allowed" comments.

Fact #3 Expect a Disney Disaster

When I first took all five children to Florida I went too early. Yes, yes I can hear you all saying now, 'What were you thinking of?!' Well I had to learn from my mistakes and now I tell others not to do it. You would have thought I would've learned my lesson from Center-Parks-Gate. But no...

When the children were aged between two and eight I thought it would be lovely and jolly for us all to go off to Florida,

Disneyland etc. Please note that at this time I was very definitely a fully-fledged BTM. LH was also still on the scene, so I took the precaution of paying a 'helper' to come with us.

It all went *really well* until we woke up in the morning to actually *go* on holiday. It was then I realised that Charley had chickenpox. Had I been a PM naturally I would have immediately cancelled the holiday and stayed at home or at least offered to stay behind and look after her. As I was a BTM, I started trying out different shades of concealer to make sure I could get her through check in.

Concealer applied off we went to the airport encountering only;

- Rosie, setting off little 'hate bombs' and turning into an even more massive control freak by analysing all information screens in the airport in order to give us best advice.

- Katie anxiously watching our faces for any signs of worry or thought. Needing to go to the toilet about 17 times an hour

- Sophie setting off little hand grenades of joy, "Oooh look Mummy, William has wet himself." Etc.

- William wetting himself a couple of times

- Charley looking pasty and hot, and reminding me I was a very BAD mother.

I can tell you now I had to pay for the first 48 hours, staying up all night looking after Charley and her chickenpox, while LH and paid 'Helper' slept through.

Once we got into Disneyland, I discovered that all five of my children were frightened of people wearing costumes. Now if you have ever been to Disneyland you will know that this is not a good place to discover that your children are scared of people in costumes. Even though we had paid over £200 to enter, we were out by lunchtime. No amount of reassurance or 'meeting Sleeping Beauty with fully exposed face' worked. Added to that the fact that Charley was still a bit 'poxy' and being looked at askance lying dismally in her pushchair, it wasn't the most successful of days.

Disney footnote: Apparently you're not a child anymore once you get past the age of 10. This is actually official because over the age of 10, you have to pay adult prices to get into Disney. This meant, that when we visited Disneyland for the second attempt three years later, Rosie, then aged 11, was able to claim she could now drive a car and vote. I also hoped this meant she thought she could leave home. But no.

Fact #4 You Will Not Be Relaxing

Therapeutic Parents learn really quickly to turn disasters into something more positive however, and I already had this skill. After experiencing this first Disney Disaster, I thought, "We have a villa, we have a pool, it is sunny, it will be lovely!"

Well it would have been lovely had I not been solely responsible for all five children. Even though LH and 'Paid Helper' were with me and technically 'helping' it only seemed to be me who spotted the child drowning in the swimming pool….twice. At one point I even jumped in to pull her out when I saw her smiling at me from underneath the water.

Following this LH and Lazy-Non-Helper told me I was 'making an unnecessary fuss'. I had interrupted their reading time next to the pool with all the splashing I believe. Lazy-Non-Helper even had the audacity to tell me that I shouldn't 'overreact' as otherwise the children would become 'scared of the water'. I asked her if she thought it was better that the children were not scared of the water so drowned instead? She huffily went back to her book.

The Lazy-Non-Helper became slightly less helpful once we went out for the day and she refused to wear a hat in 80 degrees as it would 'flatten her hair'. The resulting sunstroke laid her low for 48 hours, and she was slightly miffed that I would not cancel the trip to the aquarium to 'look after her'.

You can see how and why I became so bad-tempered so quickly in the early years.

There is also no such thing as 'sunbathing' anymore when you are on holiday with AC. Instead there is;

- sitting on the towel surrounded by beach toys, and AC throwing sand at each other

- sitting near a pool surrounded by AC playing perilous 'games'

It is not nice and it is not fun.

When you add to this the mix of children who do not want to wear suntan cream and complain it is some 'kind of abuse' if you dare to touch them with the cream, you have a recipe for a happy family day out culminating in shrieks of sunburnt pain towards the end.

Over the years I learnt that the best way to get any peace was to take my trusty headphones with me. In this way, once I knew the children could swim or they had their little lifejackets securely attached and I could lie down and watch with 'tolerant Mummy smile' firmly in place, and listen to my music. I did not have to hear;

- "Look mummy!"

- "See me jump in the pool!"

- "But it's MY turn to have the lilo!"

- Subsequent bashing noises.

Fact #5 You *Can* Have Holiday Fun with INPs

There is fun to be had by taking an Ignorant Non Parent on holiday with you. The INP thinks it's going to be jolly good fun. If you have been away before, you may allow yourself a few moments of pity and reflection on their behalf. You may be reminded of your younger, naive self, embarking on 'holiday adventures'.

On one 'enforced 'road trip' (AKA 'being lost') my INP friend asked me tensely, "Do they *ever* actually stop arguing?" *I* thought we were all trundling along the road happily in our minibus. I did not know what she was talking about as I no longer heard the arguing. I tuned in to try to see what the issue was and realised there was the usual undercurrent of;

- You are touching my seat

- No I am not- you smell

- Get off me, stinky

- You are fat

- Mu-um!

- Poo head…

…in various stages of development.

As I had retuned my listening antennae a couple of years previously, I happily informed my INP friend that this was just normal background noise, and offered her my headphones which she accepted with alacrity.

On the same holiday my INP friend thought that Charley had drowned. We were in a 'lazy river' in a theme park going round on our little rubber rings, accompanied by the usual incessant commentary from Charley Chatty.

- Are we in the swimming pool?

- I like my swimming costume

- Do you like your swimming costume?

- Why is water wet?

- Why are rubber rings round?

Suddenly Charley disappeared. A perfect, quiet relief ensued. I continued to enjoy the peace and relative silence, showing no interest or concern, (concealing any potential triggers into the bargain), as sadly I knew she would resurface shortly and the nonsense chatter flood would resume.

The INP having no such bad parenting habits, immediately started panicking and looking round frantically in the water for Charley. 30 seconds later she re surfaced smiling, "Here I am!" The INP exclaimed, "I thought you had drowned!" Charley laughed manically.

I continued surreptitiously drifting further away on my rubber ring. It was going to be a long day.

Fact #6 Skiing Holidays Will Be 'Challenging'

When I first had the inspirational idea of taking all my children skiing, I obviously had no clue. Previously, I had been away skiing with families who had securely attached children, and enjoyed *appropriate* snowball fights with structured ski lessons.

Even though the therapeutic parenting part of me carefully arranged to;

- always stay in the same apartment,

- take our own bedding and familiar items with us,

- drive to the resort to minimise plane transition trauma, -

-we still encountered a myriad of difficulties, contributing to my growing bad-temperedness and frustrations.

The first skiing holiday was naturally the most challenging as the children did not know what to expect. As LH was present (in body only) for the first holiday it took me about an hour to get them all into ski suits and ski boots. For those of you who have endured this, you will feel my pain.

By the time we had managed to leave the apartment I was already hot and sweaty, struggling to balance a plethora of ski poles and unsteady children in newly rented ski boots. We wobbled onto the snowy paths, on our way to the nursery slopes. It was as we arrived that I noticed two of the children had mysterious protrusions in the bum area of their ski suits. I 'wondered aloud' in an un-therapeutic-gritted-teeth-voice, if 'anyone might have had an accident' and needed assistance. Shortly after we all slowly made our way back to the apartment, so I could divest two of the children of their pooed in ski suits, whilst ignoring the other three complaining that they were hot.

Once we all managed to exit again, I realised that William had wet himself. It was at times like these that I had to have a word with myself about the wisdom of trying to take on these mammoth tasks. I decided it was time for us all to lie down in the snow, and then have a snowball fight, instead of going skiing.

Charley never quite got the hang of skiing. Even at the age of three she complained that her skis did not work as 'the batteries had run out'. She was horrified to discover that she was required to put in effort, in order to make them move, rather than remaining in an 'expectant downhill squat' position.

I knew we were probably in for a rough ride with Charley from this point forward. She was not naturally sporty. (My mum *still* referred to her as 'a lumpen child'). I thought the best plan was to put her into the pre-school ski lessons, thinking that she was less likely to tantrum if I was not the teacher.

One day, I travelled into town, passing overhead the nursery ski-school in a cable car on my way. As we travelled along I saw a few passengers start to smile and point. I had a déjà vu moment from the Christmas school-angel ordeal. Sure enough, as we passed over there were 20 good little 3-year-olds standing in a nice straight line, patiently waiting their turn to snow-plough sedately down the adjoining slope. There was one, purple-faced, chubby child at the side, throwing skis about and kicking ski boots off in a rage.

This tantrumming-on-the-slopes behaviour was merely a prequel for the many times in the future we would need to all stop to see the furious little spec in the distance, taking off skis and hurling them around in fury in the snow.

Katie and William were also very cautious about learning to ski. Often I would arrive at ski school to pick them up from the two hour lesson, only to find that they had been 'very cold' and had *had* to spend 1.5 hours in the ski school office drinking hot chocolate. I was very pleased that I had paid large sums of money to enable them to do this. Ski school did not last very long.

Rosie Rudey also struggled with the 'making effort' and actual 'skiing part' of skiing. As an IRT she ignored my advice that she 'might need ski gloves' and went off out skiing without them. Luckily she was with Patient Husband at the time, so when she fell over and howled in pain at the 'cold snow' on her bare hands, he was able to assist. She lay prostrate on the ground, screaming as if she had a broken leg and tricking the monitors in to placing crossed ski poles in front of her as if she had had a major accident. PH lent her his own gloves and skied on. Amazingly there was a sudden, miraculous recovery and she followed.

Whilst skiing down the mountain, on our fifth family skiing holiday, I caught up with Katie Careful who appeared to be taking off her skis. I asked her what she was doing, and she (inconceivably) replied that she was swapping her skis round onto different feet as they kept 'going the wrong way'. Although I was tempted to say something, it was better for everyone's mental health to simply ski away.

Fact #8 Birthdays Don't Combine Well with Holidays

One memorable holiday Charley's birthday was due to fall right in the middle of it. She asked me if she could invite her friends. I explained at some length that we would be in Florida and that it would be very difficult for her friends to come to a party there. She assured me that they 'would not mind' so I felt this was a good learning opportunity.

Charley began excitedly writing out the invitations and took them round all her friends. I made sure she understood that any friends coming to Florida from the UK would have to make sure they;

- had a parent with them

- provided their own villa

- paid for their own airfare.

Charley did not mind and said all her friends would not mind either. She was *very* excited about all her friends coming to Florida.

Her friends were also very excited about coming to Florida for Charley's party.

Sadly, the parents seemed less than enthusiastic. I seem to be on the receiving end of pointy-eyebrow-death-stares at the school gate. Whilst I found this quite amusing I knew that I would have to prepare for the disappointment which was bound to follow.

Fortuitously, I had friends holidaying in the same area at the same time so I made sure they were on standby just *in case* one of Charley's eight-year-old friends could not make the trip to America.

Unfortunately, one by one, the friends fell away as their inconsiderate, unreasonable parents told them they would *not* be taking them to Florida for a birthday party.

As a BTM this caused me much delight and made me even less popular. This had the unexpected bonus knock-on effect where people avoided talking to me a bit more.

Once Charley knew there would be an ice-cream cake, presents and a party along with all the other exciting things, she quickly got over her disappointment. She sent all the invitees postcards instead, but I didn't notice any thaw from the Mummy Mafia on our return.

Fact #9 'Going Away' for Christmas is a Bad Idea

One Christmas I made the reckless decision to try to combine Christmas with 'a holiday'. For those of you considering this you are either very, very brave or very, very stupid. I was the latter.

It took us 12 hours travelling to get there, crammed to the roof with the hidden and disguised Christmas presents. We went to a place called the 'Mull of Kintyre' in Scotland. There is a famous song about it by Paul McCartney. I thought it was going to be romantic and beautiful with snow almost certain to appear. Instead the 'Mist rolling in from the glen', line in the song, appeared to be remarkably appropriate. It wasn't so much that the mist rolled in from the glen, it was more that the thick fog stayed in the glen… constantly. The whole time we were there I did not see further than the end of the garden. We could have been anywhere.

The AC, out of their comfort zone, argued even more than normal. The television did not work and the cottage smelt musty and damp. We took an INP with us to 'help out'. When we returned from the holiday, the INP, although still a nonparent, she was no longer ignorant. We had managed to leave her alone in a holiday cottage for two hours with my five dysfunctional children. She did not want to have children herself after this experience.

We never went away at Christmas ever again

Fact #10 Traveling Home Is Not Fun

It appeared logical to me that a 7-year-old facing a lengthy plane journey might require some essentials for the trip. I therefore packed items in Charley's rucksack such as;

- A blanket
- A flask
- Headphones
- Spare knickers
- A book
- A comic
- A favourite teddy

These items were discarded with contempt and re packed (without my knowledge). Just after the plane had taken off, I unpacked Charley's rucksack to discover;

- 17 lip balms (assorted flavours)
- 'Best Friend' necklace (in box)
- 4 Barbie dolls (one headless)
- 3 cardboard boxes (small, empty)
- 4 small paper parasols
- Assorted costume jewelry

- Barbie nail polish

- 1 cocktail shaker (large)

(It was this last item which actually made the man sitting behind me start to cry with laughter).

My resulting top tip from this is: Make sure you can answer the question, 'Did you pack the bags yourself,' honestly.

When our assessing Social Worker spoke about 'Challenging Behaviour' I did not know that really this meant;

-One day your child may turn round to you, scream at you, hit you, call you a f****** bitch, tell you they are leaving and march off with a suitcase. This would be normally be manageable, but in the middle of Orlando International airport with four other children and an interested crowd, it can be a bit tricky to manage.

It can be even trickier to manage if another child joins in the screaming exodus and also leaves. When this happened, I was pretty much a fully-fledged Therapeutic Parent and the BTM part helped me stay strong in my 'no nonsense' approach.

I told the accompanying INP that we would be leaving immediately to go to another terminal. Ignoring her look of horror, I explained that the two escapees would be lurking nearby and stalking us. We would have no chance of finding them if they could see us, but we couldn't see them. I was pretty confident that if we disappeared they would somehow make themselves found.

Reassuring William, who had saucer eyes, that we were playing a fab game of hide and seek, we relocated to the next terminal. After a tense 20 minute wait I was tannoyed to go to the police station. With some relief, I made my way to the airport station, expecting to be arrested for child abandonment and hoping I would soon be released from custody to see my three other children again.

On arrival, the policeman pointed at the sullen, blotchy twosome and asked me "Are these your children Ma'am?" I discarded the brief fantasy of saying "No," and returning to England with just three children. I admitted they were. He asked me how come they had been 'wandering round the airport on their own,' so I told him, "Well they were very rude to me and marched off. I have three other children so I couldn't follow."

Now I must admit, at this point I became THRILLED that I was in America and not the UK. The policeman turned to my daughters and roared, "Is that RIGHT!?? Did you disrespect your MOM?!!"

I did a little mental dance of glee, enjoying the unfamiliar sensation of being backed up by a non-patronising professional. Cue much feet shuffling and mumbling from the girls. "Well if you do that again," he continued in his best stern voice, "You might be spending a l'il bit of time in my *jail*!"

Now I am not advocating this as a therapeutic parenting method, but it jolly well did the trick and was balm to my soul after years of tiptoeing around politically correct, interfering Patronising Professionals. I knew that if I had been at home we would probably have been facing a case conference to 'think about' my parenting style, at the very least.

Needless to say the girls made their way swiftly to my side and stuck like glue. Only daring to whisper a small argument once we were safely on the plane.

Once we arrived back at Heathrow, we had the added drama of lost suitcases. When I was tannoyed for the second time that day, I went to information, fully expecting to be reunited with a lost suitcase. But no. I was reunited with a child I had lost but had not yet realised was missing....

One of the stories I tell at training which always brings gratifying gasps of horror, is the day I left my children arguing at the side of the motorway.

After a 12-hour journey home through France and the Eurotunnel, accompanied by rain, sounds of arguing and fighting noises periodically punctuated by the blissful (sleeping) silence, we reached a point where we were in a solid traffic jam at 3am on the M25.

Obviously I learned very quickly as a result of this trip that you do *not* go on holiday where you are likely to be travelling during the night with overtired, arguing children.

At the time we had a 7 seater 'people carrier'. This meant that the two children sitting in the furthest backseat could not be physically reached by myself or Patient Husband.

In the rear view mirror I saw Rosie Rudey and Katie Careful punching each other in the head repeatedly, accompanied by loud screeching and screaming noises.

Being in a traffic jam on the motorway I was unable to climb out of my seat as we were moving every few seconds. Patient Husband had managed to fall asleep despite the furore around him. Situation normal then.

Suddenly I got to a point where the red mist descended. I took the next exit off the motorway, having already failed by delivering banshee like screaming at Rosie and Katie to stop punching each other. I knew therapeutic parenting statements like 'I can see you are upset,' were not going to even be heard above the indignant shrieking.

I drove up the slipway and off onto a dual carriageway pulling over at the very first opportunity. Seething with rage I marched around to the back of the car opened the boot and removed the two punching-people. They stood at the side of the road, blinking confusedly, clearly in some shock at having been extracted so quickly from the lovely, dark punching session and plonked into the cold, rainy, noisy night.

I managed to do a few seconds of calm talking but faced with mutinous glares and even slyer punching, I quickly escalated into screaming, 'THAT'S IT!!!'

As I marched back to the driver's seat, I was reminded of John Cleese losing it and hitting his car with the branches to make it go. This is where I was. In a complete rage I got in the car and pulled away.

As I drove away I looked in my rear view mirror and saw my two daughters standing at the side of the busy road getting smaller and smaller. Luckily common sense quickly got a hold of me and I slammed the brakes on and started reversing quickly back down the road. Even while doing this though, a mutinous little voice in my head was saying, 'Keep GOING!'

I have to say this is not a therapeutic parenting strategy; it's not even a very good idea. But I was a BTM who had reached her limit. Her absolute limit.

I opened the back of the people carrier and said through gritted teeth, "Get in."

I don't know if the children were shocked at having been left at the side of the road, or stunned that I had returned. They got in the car without a word. We passed the rest of the journey in blissful peace.

This is now a famous story in our family folklore. "Do you remember when Mum lost it and abandoned us at the side of the motorway?"

PART SIX:

IT'S OK IN THE END (USUALLY)

Happy News #1 Revenge is mine

The children have all grown up! Oh deep joy! No more gouges in furniture, persuading stinky teens out of bed, negotiating hard for small jobs to be done, working out what the note from school actually *means,* and everything else in earlier chapters.

You remember all those times when your child;

- Wouldn't get dressed

- Wore appallingly eaten clothing

- Lay on the floor of the supermarket at crucial 'movement needed' time

- Wore embarrassing clothes out for dinner because it was 'the fashion'?

Well... now it's *your* time!

On one such occasion, I offered to take Sophie- still-a bit Spikey, Katie-no-longer-Careful and Rosie-not-Rudey out for a bit of shopping and on to the cinema. As they all lived independently, I picked them up from their homes and off we set. I could sense a bit of tension, which initially I put down to the fact that there had been some discussion about who should sit in the front. I had dressed casually, wearing my favourite tie-dye multi-coloured neon hoodie. The reason for the anxiety became clear on exiting the car.

I heard Katie whisper to Sophie, "Don't say anything... at least she hasn't got the matching shoes on!" I had a little smirk to myself, remembering all my similar therapeutic 'picking your battles' moments over the years.

We went into a shoe shop, as Katie was expecting her second child and I had offered to get her some comfy shoes. While we were choosing I heard an exchange between two of the girls, and thought there may be cross words. Without thinking about it I automatically went into the old 'hysterical playfulness' and said, "Do you know the new way you have to test shoes?" Cue some puzzled looks and a couple of apprehensive glances between them. After all, they were with Mum, *and* in a shopping mall. Anything could happen..... "Well," I continued, "You have to test them by doing Irish jigs in them now!" I then proceeded to hum some Irish music loudly, with arms ramrod straight and performing some River-dance moves;

- Katie muttered, "Oh my days!" and moved away quickly.

- Sophie went bright red and pretended to look at some interesting shoes far away.

- Rosie merely tutted and rolled her eyes.

I then remembered they were quite well regulated now and probably didn't need my 'playful' intervention.

The shoe-shop assistant eyed me warily as I put the scuffed shoes back in their box.

Happy News #2 Therapeutic Parenting Builds Resilience!

When the children were living at home, we had an incident most days. In the early years, these incidents would have floored me, by the end, we were so used to them that they didn't really make any impact.

I was chatting to my friend on the phone one day about life in general, work etc. At the end of the conversation I mentioned in passing that my dog had gone off down a fox-hole that day and we had had to wait two hours for her to resurface, narrowly avoiding calling the fire service. Her response to this information was, "Oh my God! I can't believe that! If that had happened to me today I would have been so traumatised. It would have been the FIRST thing I would have told you!"

I was a bit taken aback at this. Then I realised that just as alcoholics have to drink more and more in order to get drunk, I now only felt major stress if there was a culmination of events, or at least one or two tragedies and dramas very close together.

When the electricity board smashed our fences down, dug a fourteen-foot trench in our garden in the middle of the night and then left electricity cables exposed for 10 days. I was a bit put out because the dogs could get out of the garden. My neighbours were incandescent with rage.... For weeks!

I mentioned earlier in the book how I once had a stroke mid meeting and the social worker failed to notice. I was admitted to hospital where I languished for a week. I spent most of the time wandering the corridors of the hospital. I would write my mobile number on the whiteboard, tell the nurses to ring me if a doctor appeared and needed to see me, and off I went. I discharged myself a week later and got on with my life.

I think it is excellent news that traumatised children help you to cope with just about anything.

Happy News # 3 BTMs Make Patient Grandmothers

At the time of writing this I have three grandchildren. The third was born today! As a very BTM and Therapeutic Parent, I cannot describe the joy it brings having securely attached grandchildren.

The therapeutic parenting techniques work like a dream on them. I have time to marvel at leaves falling off trees, talk about the seasons, wonder if babies' heads will stay purple, discuss whether or not Mummy would indeed 'like a bogey as a present'.

Nonsense chatter is a fun pastime… because I know it will stop when she goes home.

My patience and tolerance knows no bounds. My children stare at me open mouthed in wonder. Probably thinking 'Who is this woman and what have you done with our mother?'

It's amazing how much simpler life is when you do not have to be somewhere on a tight deadline. Now I know for sure that school will not be contacting me about anything at all and we have no social workers in our lives.

I don't really know why children say my grandchildren are difficult sometimes….

Happy News #4 You Get Whatever Car You Want (probably)

So I ditched the people carrier and the 4x4 with the saved seats and the designated spaces with crusty food. I bought a lovely whizzy 2 seater BMW with *no room* in the back for Arguing Children. It was LOVELY!! I couldn't give people lifts or have more than one person in the car with me at once. Arguing became impossible.....

.....And then the grandchildren started arriving... well, personally I think they *are* safer in our 4x4......

Happy News #5 AC Strengthen Relationships

For many years, my PH would come home and find his BTM wife in one of three states;

1. crying in the corner.

2. upbeat with hysterical playfulness in full flow.

3. mentally or physically absent

Because he is indeed a Patient Husband, in the first year, he would often ask how my day had been. This is an error. If you ask a BTM how the day has been, it cannot go well from this point on.

It is better to make a cup of tea smile sympathetically and pat her shoulder in an understanding way. Do *not*, under any circumstances offer to solve any problems.

We have enjoyed a long and happy marriage because my husband took this advice on board at an early stage. For his part he said it worked well for him because the 'pressure was off' and all he had to do was make the cup of tea and wear a sympathetic face. Much easier than trying to solve the problem about what to do with William who had gone missing, stolen £500 or whacked his sister over the head with a tennis racket.

With help from PH we did indeed get to the day when we all skied down the mountain together. I had a brief happy Good-Tempered-Mother moment, where I turned around to see the children skiing in an orderly fashion, like a little snake behind us. There was no arguing as all their attention was taken up with staying upright and following the person in front. In a rare moment of cooperation, they shouted warnings to each other about icy patches and bumps.

Oh the joy!

Happy News #6 Holidays Are Now Holidays!

The Arguing Children had all left home and were welcome and occasional visitor, so PH and I treated ourselves to a nice cruise.

During the cruise, PH noted that I had managed to retain a large measure of BTM, which was especially in evidence when unsuspecting passengers attempted to be sociable with me.

I know at times I came across as rude, anti-social and judgemental, so perhaps this explains Fortune-cookie-gate.

In the Chinese restaurant on the ship, following a nice meal, we were both given fortune cookies. PH's read 'You are courteous and charming.' (True).

Mine - EMPTY!!! Seriously?

Clearly I had no fortune....

PH helpfully suggested they kept certain cookies 'vacant to avoid upsetting rude, intolerant people.'

He may have had a point.

Afterword-

How I became a Bad-Tempered Mother

It is not my fault I am a BTM. It is the Government's. Here is my excuse.

Several years after adopting an assumed-to-be-tricky-boy, the social workers were very pleased with themselves that the little boy was 'settling down nicely' and had 'probably forgotten all about his horrific start in life'. They patted each other on the back and exclaimed with delight about how 'well placed' the little boy had been with his very loving, good and patient mother.

One day the nearly tricky boy, started to become an 'actual Tricky Boy'. This happened because he had a 'disorder' which made him do naughty things. No one was allowed to say it was naughty though, so instead they said things like 'interesting' and 'sad'.

His G&P Mother took him to see lots of important therapists and doctors. Mostly the therapists and doctors argued amongst themselves about the 'Best Thing To Do' and 'The Most Important Disorder'.

The Nearly Tricky Boy swore at his G&P Mother trying out the 'interesting words' he had heard at nursery. Words he had heard from somewhere, but he wasn't quite sure where. Words that made him feel wobbly inside. The G&P Mother gently chastised her wobbly boy and suggested kinder words to use instead.

The now Tricky Boy continued to try different methods of annoying and tormenting his mother, who slowly but surely started to become bad- tempered. The little boy did not *mean* to annoy and torment his mother. He just wanted to make sure she did not forget about him. Like his last mother had.

The G&P Mother asked the Wise and Knowledgeable Social Worker to help her, as the Tricky Boy seemed to have some problems she didn't understand. The Social Worker was 'Very Busy Indeed' but sent through a pair of roller skates, a parenting manual and a shiny reward chart.

The roller skates did not help. The not very G&P Mother wished she could put them on and skate very far away, very quickly.

The increasingly desperate G&P Mother considered other methods of disciplining her child. In the supermarket, he threw a tantrum because she would not give him the unhealthy snack. Checkout assistants, Perfect Mothers and Ignorant Non Parents stared at her accusingly, while she made hopeless and inadequate sounding noises.

She decided to try using 'The Naughty Step' as Super Nanny said this was a good idea. Her Health Visitor told her she *must* use 'The Naughty Step' as this was 'the best way to deal with tricky children'.

The first time the (now) BTM used The Naughty Step, she couldn't bear to see her little boy punching himself in the face, so she stopped it straight away and worried about telling the Health Visitor that she couldn't do it.

When the Tricky Boy went to nursery he got upset one day because the nursery assistant refused to give him a 'goodbye kiss'.

The BTM told the nursery that the Tricky Boy had a 'disorder' and didn't understand why he couldn't have a goodbye kiss. She explained that he was even naughtier, now he that he was also angry and sad.

She asked why his nursery assistant could not give him a goodbye kiss. The Important Nursery Head told the BTM that it was a 'Child Protection' issue and that these kinds of things 'Damaged Children for Life.'

The BTM enquired as to whether the Important Nursery Head, (with her years of training), believed her son was more likely to be 'Damaged for Life' by getting a peck on the cheek from his nursery assistant, who he loved, or rejected by her in case the kiss was an unlikely, disguised, sex attack.

The Important Nursery Head gave the BTM a 'Paddington Hard Stare,' and made a note on her file that she was a 'Difficult Parent' and possibly a BTM.

Two years later, at infants' school, the Tricky Boy was taught that adults *cannot be trusted*. He learned this through strangers coming to the school, and telling him he must not trust strangers in case they put him in their car and steal him. The Tricky Boy had nightmares about being stolen. He wondered if in fact, he had already *been* stolen.

The Tricky Boy's teachers seemed to change a lot. One day he did not recognise his teacher as she had new glasses on. He hid under the table until his BTM came and sorted it all out. The Teacher thought the BTM was 'Making a Fuss.'

When she was a fully-fledged BTM, and her son was a fully-fledged Tricky Boy, the BTM stopped to consider her options. Her old-parent-instinct was to send this child to his room or shout loudly at him.

The Tricky Boy did not seem to think he had to take too much notice of her anymore. The BTM asked the Teacher if she could help. The Teacher told the BTM that her son 'wouldn't remember anything and should have settled down by now.' She offered to put reminders in the homeschool diary about doing homework. The BTM said she couldn't do homework as well as it was too difficult to manage on top of everything else. She said even if she shouted loudly at her Tricky Boy, he would not do his homework.

The Teacher told the BTM that 'The Government' says she must *not* shout loudly at her child because she will 'Damage Him For Life. The BTM asked what she should be doing to help her Tricky Boy be less tricky. The Teacher said she was Very Busy Indeed, but offered to put the BTM forward for parenting classes.

The next day, the Teacher asked the Tricky Boy to bring in a photo of him as a baby as the whole class were going to look at them and discuss them. The Tricky Boy had never seen a photo of him as a baby. He didn't want to think about all the bad things that had happened to him when he was little. When the children brought their photos in, the Tricky Boy started ripping them all up. The Teacher was Very Cross Indeed and told the Tricky Boy that he was now a Very Naughty Boy and had to go outside on his own to think about his behaviour.

The Very Naughty Boy was very angry and sad and started breaking things and shouting. He remembered all the bad swear words and used them all up at once on the Teacher.

The Important Head Teacher sat the now Very Naughty Boy down to talk about his behaviour with him. She asked the Tricky Boy why he had done the things he had done. The Very Naughty Boy hit the Important Head Teacher, who then told the BTM that her son was 'too naughty' to stay in school with all the good children and had to stay at home as a punishment for a week.

The BTM wondered who was being punished, and asked 'difficult questions' about the baby photos fiasco.

The Important Head Teacher wrote down some more notes about the BTM and her 'attitude'.

When he was 15, the Very Naughty Boy decided he was not going to go to school at all anymore. By now the BTM knew quite a lot about therapeutic parenting, but unfortunately she was having a bad day. She shouted at him and told him he 'jolly well was going to school,' but the Very Naughty Boy merely asked, "What are you going to do about it?"

The Bad-Tempered (and desperate for respite) Mother, phoned the school and told them that her son was refusing to go to school. The school were secretly relieved as they considered him to be a Very Naughty Boy. They were also pleased that they could use his specially allocated teaching assistant, for some other tricky children instead. Nevertheless, the school told her it would 'Damage Her Child for Life' if he did not return to school immediately.

The BTM said she would not interfere with whatever consequences the school wanted to put in place, but that she really needed them to at least organise a meeting to discuss a way forward.

The school told her they were Very Busy Indeed but that she needed to get her son to school as otherwise she would 'Damage Her Child for Life'.

The BTM asked the school what she should do. She mentioned some good ideas about therapeutic parenting, but the Head Teacher stuck his fingers in his ears.

The school said they could not advise, but that they would report her and take her to court if the Very Naughty Boy did not return to school.

A month later the BTM was very bad-tempered indeed when she received a letter from 'The Government' telling her she had to go to parenting classes so she could learn how to be an 'Effective Parent'.

The BTM tried to tell The Government, via the Social Worker that she had to do different parenting as her son had a 'disorder' and needed therapeutic parenting. She asked the Social Workers if they had any training on Therapeutic Parenting, but the Social Workers only had time to make baffled, patronising faces.

At the parenting classes, the BTM was surprised to find that she had a lovely time meeting all the other bad-tempered parents. They all snorted and chuckled together derisively, when the childless Patronising-Perfect-Parenting-'Expert' told them how they must sit down their Very Naughty children (now Incredibly Rude Teenagers), and;

- Talk to them about their behaviour

- Bring in a reward chart

- Listen respectfully

- Be more of a friend

The bad-tempered parents pointed out that their Incredibly Rude Teenagers would sneer at them on their way out of the back door.

The Patronising-Perfect-Parenting-Expert explained that the Bad-Tempered Parents merely needed to explain to their 'misunderstood' young person, (she didn't like them using the term IRT), that they would like them to remain at home so they could 'have a nice chat.'

The BTM pointed out that her IRT was 6'2", quite wide and very angry. She was 5'4" and often on her own. The Patronising-Perfect-Parenting-Expert told her to stop being so negative.

When she got home, the BTM tried to sit her IRT down to 'have a chat.' He swore a lot, put his fist through the door, and then walked out. He didn't come home all night. The BTM phoned the police.

The police brought the IRT back the next morning and told the BTM that she 'must not let him run away again.' The BTM asked if she should 'lock him in.' The policeman looked shocked and said this was 'not allowed,' as it could 'Damage Her Child for Life.'

The BTM asked whether she should try to grab him to stop him running off. The policeman made another shocked face and said this was 'not allowed either'. The BTM asked how she could stop her Incredibly Rude, (big, strong) Teenager from running away. The policeman said it was 'not his problem.'

Four weeks later, the IRT stole a lot of money from his neighbour. The BTM phoned the police to tell them. The Youth Offending Team came to visit. They decided that a bit of adventure would be good for the IRT. They started to take him rock climbing and sailing. The BTM tried to tell the Youth Offending Team that her IRT had had lots of lovely holidays and treats already. The BTM asked how her son is learning not to steal.

Two weeks later the Very Naughty IRT stole a lot more money from the BTM. The BTM reported it to his Youth Offending Team. They said it was 'Very Serious Indeed' and that it would have to go to court.

The Very Naughty IRT went to court. His BTM went with him to support him. The court was very cross with the IRT AND his BTM. They gave the BTM a fine to pay back the person her IRT had stolen from.

"But," protested the BTM, "He stole from ME!"

The Judge said that was 'not his problem.' He made an order for the BTM to pay all the money her IRT had stolen from *her*, back to the court.

The Very Naughty IRT was very happy. He had learned that he could do whatever he wanted and would still have a nice reward. If he stole off his parents or neighbours, his parents have to pay it back, even to *themselves!* He thought this was very funny. He enjoyed the rock climbing and canoeing provided by the Youth Offending Team. They were very good at talking to him about his feelings. The Very Naughty IRT had quickly learned that he could easily get the worker from there to put his name down first for all the exciting trips. All he had to do was make a sad face and say how much he regretted everything.

Sometimes the Youth Offending Team man got a bit cross because the Very Naughty IRT would not go to the office for his appointments. On these occasions, the Youth Offending Man would pop his head round the door of the Very Naughty IRT's bedroom and do a tick on his chart to say he had 'seen him'. The Very Naughty IRT did not even have to get out of bed. He thought this was a great game.

A month later the BTM and her Patient Husband were told by 'The Government' that they would get a big fine if they didn't make their Very Naughty IRT go to school and stop stealing. The BTM (quite rightly) pointed out that The Government had removed every possible effective consequence she had ever tried to implement, and not listened to her good ideas about therapeutic parenting.

The Government told her it was not their problem, but hers. They did not even have the grace to shuffle their feet and look a bit embarrassed.

Finally, the BTM uses the last of her savings to find a Therapist-Who-Has-A-Clue. The Therapist-Who Has-A-Clue knows all about attachment and what happens when children are neglected. He knows what needs to happen to help the BTM's son. He writes letters to the school, social services, the court and the Youth Offending Team.

Eventually there is a Big Important Meeting. By now the BTM and her Very Naughty IRT are able to look at each other and even smile a bit sometimes. After the Big Important Meeting, her son leaves the room to have a cigarette.

The people in the meeting are amazed at what the Therapist-Who-Has-A-Clue has explained to them all. They exclaim to each other, "**But He Looks So Normal!**"

Acknowledgements

In writing this book I have relied heavily on our experiences as a family and what we have learned together over the years.

I would like to thank all the Therapeutic Parents on our 'Therapeutic Parents' Facebook Group who never fail to inspire me every day. You are all still going through it and seem to have so much more patience and tolerance than me!

I also need to say a big thank you to my staunch Ignorant Non Parent, Catherine, who helped me hugely when the children were young, and Lazy Husband was at his laziest.

Although social workers have had a bit of a rough ride in this book one of my staunchest allies, Margaret, is the best Social Worker I ever met and helped me in our darkest days, more than she will ever know.

The team at Inspire Training Group help me to keep helping all the parents, social workers and teachers we work with. Rosie, Sarah, Sair, Hazel, Jodie and Jane have enabled our company to become successful, but much more importantly, to help parents achieve better outcomes for their traumatised children.

To my husband Ray, who has been my rock and my steadying hand, thank you. You did not have to join our family all those years ago and you didn't have to stay, but we are all so glad and grateful that you did.

To my children, Rosie, Katie, William, Sophie and Charley I love you all and thank you from the bottom of my heart for helping me to (mostly) overcome my bad-temperedness and to become a better person. I am so proud of each and every one of you.

And finally to my parents, without whom, I would not have had secure attachments, and could never have understood all the things I do now.

Lots of Love

Sarah XXXXX

21092351R00110

Printed in Poland
by Amazon Fulfillment
Poland Sp. z o.o., Wrocław